GUNS&AMMO
Guide to
AR-15s

GUNS&AMMO

Guide to AR-15s

A COMPREHENSIVE GUIDE TO BLACK GUNS

EDITORS OF GUNS & AMMO

INTRODUCTION BY ERIC R. POOLE

Skyhorse Publishing

Visit our website at www.skyhorsepublishing.com.

10 9 8 7 6 5 4 3 2

Library of Congress Cataloging-in-Publication Data is available on file.

Cover design by Tom Lau
Cover photo credits: Rock River Arms and High Standard

Print ISBN: 978-1-5107-1310-9
Ebook ISBN: 978-1-5107-1316-1

Printed in China

TABLE OF CONTENTS

PART IV: TESTS & TACTICS

INTRODUCTION

My fondness for the AR-15 began with an indoctrinated intimacy during basic training. I often had to sleep with my rack-grade Colt M16A2 and I had to give it a girl's name—Lucy. At all times, she was in my possession or properly secured. I was at Parris Island a few weeks already before receipt of the 20-inch barreled beauty. Once the armory issued the M16 web sling and its cleaning gear, each recruit was expected to memorize the serial number. Strangely enough, I became so familiar with my rifle that I learned how to spot any scar or shiny edge well enough to quickly pick it out in a stack. That's a skill that saved valuable time when a green belt drill instructor was breathing down my neck.

Just like any serviceman, I learned its manual of arms, how to march with it, and field strip it for maintenance. Even before moving to the rifle range, I was spending an hour cleaning it each night before hitting the rack. And every night, I joined my platoon in reciting our creed:

This is my rifle. There are many like it, but this one is mine. My rifle is my best friend. It is my life. I must master it as I must master my life. My rifle, without me, is useless. Without my rifle, I am useless. I must fire my rifle true. I must shoot straighter than my enemy who is trying to kill me. I must shoot him before he shoots me. I will . . .

My rifle and myself know that what counts in this war is not the rounds we fire, the noise of our burst, nor the smoke we make. We know that it is the hits that count. We will hit . . .

My rifle is human, even as I, because it is my life. Thus, I will learn it as a brother. I will learn its weaknesses, its strength, its parts, its accessories, its sights and its barrel. I will ever guard it against the ravages of weather and damage as I will ever guard my legs, my arms, my eyes and my heart against damage. I will keep my rifle clean and ready. We will become part of each other. We will . . .

Before God, I swear this creed. My rifle and myself are the defenders of my country. We are the masters of our enemy. We are the saviors of my life. So be it, until victory is America's and there is no enemy, but peace!

After thirteen weeks on Parris Island, I left with a coveted expert badge and a fidelity to the controversial black rifle. Perhaps if I had gone off to war and spent a number of uncomfortable nights lying beside a wooden behemoth, I wouldn't be so fond of Eugene Stoner's approach. The M16 served me faithfully and provided a foundation of experience by which I judge all other modern battle rifles, and every AR I own feels like a unique piece of that lineage. Just as modern manufacturing technology progresses and feedback flows from the frontlines, each year I anxiously await the plethora of new products exploiting the rifle's modularity. I never expect that any of us will live to see the true potential of our beloved AR-15 fulfilled.

As you'll see in the pages of this book, we showcase the history of the AR with a few stories from the *Guns & Ammo* archive. We also cover topics like defensive features, ammo, components, and tactics. There are chapters like Kyle E. Lamb's coverage of offensive versus shooting stances; Wayne van Zwoll's deep-dive into backup AR sights; and Patrick Sweeney's field test of various ARs to see which can withstand the most wear and tear. We wanted to represent a cross-section of all things AR-related, and we hope you find the features in the *Guns & Ammo Guide to AR-15s* interesting and useful.

Eric R. Poole

PART I
DEFENSE FEATURES

READY TO ARM

IT'S TIME TO RETHINK HOME SECURITY.

When the alarm sounds, a text message usua[l] follows a few seconds later. If that alarm co[n] tinues more than two minutes, I get a pho[ne] call from ADT. The polite operator on the oth[er] end is nowhere near my house, but he asks [if] there is reason to believe a home invasion [is] taking place or if a member of my family m[ay] have opened a door without disarming t[he] security system. (Which is usually the cas[e.]) Now I cautiously inspect my house wi[th] gun in hand as I locate my family membe[rs] and check the doors and windows. Abo[ut] a year ago, a burglary was attempted wh[ile] I was stuck in an airport. Police eventua[lly] responded about 30 minutes after I gave AD[T] the OK to send them. Not long after, a frie[nd] down the road was robbed of many perso[nal] effects—and a gun. It was a deeply disturb[ing] experience. I hate to admit that it took su[ch] unexpected measures to initiate me to a[rm] and better protect my family and property[.]

BY ERIC R. POOLE
PHOTOS BY SEAN UTLE[Y]

I keep the forty-dollar-a-month home security system active, but I view it more as a warning device, much like a smoke detector. The high-pitch squelch from either is enough to wake me up at night. I used to be the guy who slept with a pistol in the nightstand, but for home defense I've come to prefer an AR.

THE HOME DEFENSE AR

As a victim of an attempted home invasion, I can attest that the sounding of an alarm doesn't always scare off the man in a mask like TV commercials would have you believe. However, the AR isn't the perfect home defense solution for everyone either. Shooting a rifle in closed quarters requires careful consideration, specific handling and is extremely painful to the ears. If you don't select ammunition with the same level of diligence, the wrong bullet can tear through into a nearby room or neighboring home with unintended consequences. I've participated in a few wallboard-penetration tests designed to simulate the structure of a home and can tell you that a 55-grain .223 FMJ can penetrate and exit more than five walls placed 15 feet apart. Frangible and polymer-tipped bullets do a better job of breaking up and dumping velocity quickly, but you should test this for yourself and become aware of your chosen home defense setup. And when you're sweeping doors and hallways in the attempt to secure loved ones or even to escape, rifles with lengthy barrels can easily bump into furniture and other home décor, giving away your position to the intruder or impeding movement toward an exit. It all happens faster than police can respond.

This isn't a sales pitch. I take matters of personal safety very seriously. Your eyes tend to focus on a threat in a stressful situation, and you can lose perspective of the sights on the gun you may have in your hand. I can't speak for you, but I know it's much more probable that a bullet or bullets will strike the intended target(s) more assuredly when I'm using an AR platform than a handgun. When shooting a pistol quickly in low light, I tend to lose optimal sight alignment after the first shot. I don't have the same issues with an AR because, when the stock is in my shoulder, I'm looking over the top of the rifle and the muzzle is far enough out that my support hand instinctively points at the central mass I need to hit. Self-defense isn't a precision sport, but it does require probable hits and speed to survive. It's all about getting enough rounds pumped into a target until it no longer presents a threat to you or your loved ones.

ENTER DANIEL DEFENSE

The Daniel Defense ISR deserves your attention. It's chambered for .300 Blackout and

> ## [The ISR] met a need that I felt wasn't in the marketplace, **the need for a suppressed AR with a shorter barrel.**

Photos by Sean Utley

comes suppressed. Just one two-hundred-dollar tax stamp gets you a short-barreled rifle fitted with a permanently attached suppressor. Well, that's after you fork over $3,200 for the Integrally Suppressed Rifle (ISR) in .300 Blackout. I suppose you could argue that the savings for a second tax stamp isn't a make-or-break decision for the person who can afford a $3,000 suppressed rifle. But let's take a step back.

In the states that allow a law-abiding citizen to own a short-barreled rifle (SBR) and suppressor, two tax stamps are required. One stamp goes with the SBR, the other with the detachable suppressor. The key word in that last sentence is "detachable," which is how Daniel Defense has managed to reduce the ATF paperwork. For residents of states such as Michigan, where suppressors are legal but SBRs are not, the ISR is the perfect solution because the overall length of barrel with its permanently attached suppressor is 16.145 inches.

I recently evaluated a DDM4 for "Guns & Ammo" that featured a 10.3-inch barrel chambered in .300 Blackout. It's got the same barrel as the one used on the ISR, only one had an AAC suppressor adaptor affixed to its muzzle. Part of the intent of that article was to illustrate the performance of both subsonic and supersonic loads—with and without a suppressor attached. I used an Advanced Armament Corp. 762-SDN-6 for suppressed testing, which added seven inches to that rifle's overall length. It certainly is a better alternative for home defense than attaching a suppressor to a typical AR with 16-inch barrel.

There are a few minor considerations when trying to adapt a rifle that's not going to be dedicated to operating with a suppressor. First, running .300 Blackout can be tricky in a rifle that allows you to use subsonic and supersonic ammunition interchangeably with or without a suppressor attached. You'll find that most .300 Blackout rifles don't run reliably with subsonic ammunition if they are unsuppressed, and shooting supersonic ammo can sometimes over-gas a rifle with suppressor attached. So how does a company ensure that its customers are getting the best possible performance from a subsonic .300 Blackout load? The only solution I can think of is to own a rifle that's devoted to suppressed use.

If I would have known about the ISR ahead of its introduction at the 2013 SHOT Show, it would have been included in "Book of the AR-15: Blackout Edition." Although most of this book's contributors are worn out from

testing Blackout in an earlier article, the ISR can't be ignored. Even a newcomer to AR-type rifles can appreciate its virtues for not having to memorize multiple trajectories for different loads or needing to rezero for impact shifts that result when you remove and later reattach the suppressor.

PIXIE DUST

Lee Thompson, ISR project engineer for Daniel Defense, brought me up to speed and said, "I started initial development last March 2012. [The ISR] met a need that I felt wasn't in the marketplace, the need for a suppressed AR with shorter barrel. I presented the idea to the engineer group, who are a bunch of gun guys. Then it was shown to Marty Daniel. He had already been thinking along the same lines. The suppressor needed to attach to the gas block, and we needed to develop an optimal gas configuration. We went with a pistol-length gas system because we have to have so much of the barrel inside the suppressor."

Daniel Defense decided to stay with its 10.3-inch, cold hammer forged barrel attached to the upper by means of the standard MFR barrel nut. The barrel is made of 4150 chrome-moly vanadium steel, given the .300 AAC chamber and treated with a nitride salt bath. The ISR utilizes a standard bolt and bolt carrier group, as well as an H buffer and standard carbine spring. Daniel Defense experimented with an H2 buffer, but determined that it wasn't necessary for anything but the hottest loads.

As mentioned, the overall length of the barrel, to include the suppressor, is 16.145

Daniel Defense DDM4 ISR-300

TYPE	Direct impingement, semiautomatic, integrally suppressed
CALIBER	.300 AAC Blackout
BARREL	16.145 in. (10.3 in. barrel w/ permanently attached gas block and suppressor), cold hammer forged, 1:8 twist
OVERALL LENGTH	31.25 in. (collapsed), 34.75 in. (extended)
WEIGHT	7.6 lbs.
HANDGUARD	Daniel Defense Modular Float Rail (MFR) 12.0
STOCK	Magpul MOE, black
GRIP	A2
SELECTOR	Two-position
TRIGGER	Mil-Spec
MAGAZINE	Magpul PMAG 30 rds.
MUZZLE DEVICE	Daniel Defense ISR, stainless steel, monolithic baffle core, nondetachable
SIGHTS	Daniel Defense A1.5 removable fixed, elevation-adjustable post (front), windage-adjustable aperture (rear)
MSRP	$3,044 standard, $3,198 for Mil Spec + model (does not include $200 tax stamp)
MANUFACTURER	Daniel Defense 866-554-4867 danieldefense.com

inches. The suppressor itself is a little over 11¼ inches, which means that nearly five inches of the suppressor is sleeved over the barrel's exterior. Interestingly, this provides plenty of time and volume for gas to vent without degrading performance for follow-up shots. Because escaping gas blows back over the barrel, there isn't as much backpressure that returns down the bore.

"We tapered the gas port and optimized it for the various .300 Blackout loads until we hit a happy medium," Thompson adds. "We knew customers would want to run both subsonic and supersonic loads through it, so we had to develop everything to keep it from being undergassed or overgassed."

Daniel Defense had a functional prototype by early October 2012. Most of the testing up to that point was done by computer simulation, so engineers didn't have to go back and forth to

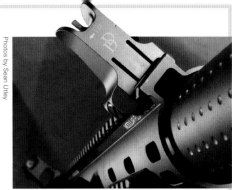

The Daniel Defense A1.5 sights are a one-hundred-twenty-dollar investment as a stand-alone sight system or to back up an optic. They simply slide on either end of the top rail and are secured by a flathead screw.

the drawing board. The result was an entirely new gas block and a stainless steel suppressor with monolithic baffle designed specifically for the ISR.

The magic behind the ISR is that the gas block is mounted with a spiral roll pin and carefully welded to the barrel, and the suppressor is given a left-hand thread and then welded directly to the custom gas block. But simply firing up a torch doesn't accurately describe the precision that permanently unites these three components. Maintenance is easy since the baffle core is removable using a provided tool.

"We were lucky," says Thompson. "The baffle design was really good from the start and only required minor tweeks as we developed the ISR. We spent most of our time perfecting the gas system. We were looking for 700 or 750 rounds per minute using subsonic ammo and 850 to 900 using super. We didn't want go over 900. We know that there are functional issues when you get near or go over a grand, especially on SBRs."

Though chambered in .300, you can still fit 30 rounds of Blackout in a typical 5.56 magazine.

FORM MEETS FUNCTION

Before testing the ISR-300 on a private range in Indiana, I took note of its configuration. The ISR includes the Modular Float Rail (MFR) 12.0, which offers adaptability through a combination of three-inch Picatinny rail sections. As is trending these days, the user gets to determine where and where not to have rails on the forend. This is an improved design for the ISR relieved underneath to accept the removable rail panels and other MFR accessories. The rail-mounted QD attachment point is also new for the MFR 12.0.

The upper receiver is Mil-Spec, and its flat-top displays indexing marks for reference when attaching optics. Inside the chamber area I found M4 feed ramps. The lower is Mil-Spec with an enhanced flare given to the magazine well. And if you look at the rear of the receiver, you'll find a quick-detach (QD) swivel attachment point.

Even with suppressor attached, the ISR only weighs 7.6 pounds. It balances a little forward toward the muzzle, but isn't so muzzle heavy that it's awkward to handle. Daniel Defense obviously digs Magpul products, because you'll notice a Magpul MOE adjustable stock, winter triggerguard and even magazine. The stock collapsed gives the ISR an overall length of just 31¼ inches, 34¾ inches when extended. You can't help but notice that the Magpul kit adds a sense of quality to the entire package.

Two ISRs were provided for testing. One of them had fired just north of 5,000 rounds without failure at the 2013 SHOT Show Media Day in Las Vegas. As I dispensed of randomly mixed 110-grain and 208-grain Hornady staggered in multiple magazines, I came to realize the effort applied to developing the gas system to make sure the ISR would cycle both subsonic and supersonic loads. Each shot sounded like punching keys on a typewriter. When you mix loads like this, it's neat to actually see how reliable a gun functions regardless of the pressures.

All of my function testing was done on an auto lower, but when I set up for accuracy testing I used a commercially configured semiauto lower with right-hand-oriented controls.

The very best group I fired from the newer of the two rifles measured 1.08 inches, and I fired more than 50 groups from a supported prone position for evaluating its accuracy. The ISR-300 is not a sub-MOA gun, and it doesn't need to be if we're talking about using it for personal defense. If you're only interested in

Performance

	American Eagle 220-gr. OTM	ATK (Federal Prototype) 220-gr. OTM	Hornady 110-gr. V-MAX	Hornady 208-gr. A-MAX	Remington Express 220-gr. OTM	Remington Premier 125-gr. Accutip
Velocity (fps)						
	890	884	2,246	958	914	2,135
Standard Deviation						
	22	20	45	28	15	25
Extreme Spread (fps)						
	60	47	116	65	39	54
Best Group (in.)						
	2.08	1.19	2.06	1.49	1.08	1.23
Avg. Group (in.)						
	2.93	1.76	2.48	2.58	1.80	1.88

The ISR arrives equipped with a few Magpul treatments like the PMAG, the adjustable MOE stock and an enhanced winter triggerguard. The Modular Float Rail is thin and readily accepts rail sections. Two ISRs were evaluated at 100 yards, and neither could average one MOA groups or less. Using Remington loads, these targets represent the closest that bullet holes came to touching.

Photos by Sean Utley

the ISR-300 for what it does on a range at 100 yards, don't expect groups tighter than 1½ and 2½ inches, depending on your ability and the ammunition you choose. I only tested the ISR for accuracy at 100 because that is what the gun publication industry has convinced many readers to look for when reading a review. If you're engaging a violent intruder from across the room in your house, you're not going to miss with the ISR for lack of performance.

THE TAKEAWAYS

Others companies have released integrally suppressed ARs, but with the ISR-300 you just need one tax stamp.

Regarding home defense, the ISR addresses major concerns with using an SBR indoors. SBRs are loud and can throw a bright muzzle flash, but they are ideal for moving around in a close-quarters environment. Though similar in length to a common AR with 16-inch barrel, the ISR-300 won't give up your night vision or deafen those around you if you have to pull the trigger.

"Everyone assumes that you buy a can for a 5.56 and it's going to be as quiet as what you hear in an action movie," says Jordan Hunter, Daniel Defense director of marketing. "The .300 is such a popular load, and it's as quiet as an HK MP5 SD. That's impressive. It just made sense to start the ISR program with a .300, but the future does include other offerings. A 5.56 is on the table, as well as a two-tax-stamp version with a removable suppressor. You might even see our own line of suppressors."

The only suggestion I provided at the conclusion of this evaluation was that a better trigger is needed and to add a heat shield, particularly near the muzzle end of the MFR 12.0 handguard. I had fired more than 500 rounds through just one gun, and after two or three mag dumps, the ISR's handguard was too hot to grab near the end. Many users might not shoot enough to notice, but some will.

I looked across the table at Thompson, the engineer, and asked, "What are you thinking about?" He replied, "I'm still going home at night staring at the ceiling and trying to come up with ways to make it better. If I was ever happy, I think I'd be doing something wrong."

The ISR-300 is everything you need in a home defense rifle. The three-thousand-dollar price can be discouraging, but for the security it provides, think of it as a once-in-a-lifetime purchase. There's nothing to regret if the day comes when you actually need it.

VERSATILE DEFENDER

AN ARGUMENT FOR ADVANCED AR CARBINES IN THE HOME.

Shotguns have been the gold standard for home defense—and for good reason. At across-the-room distances there are few that can bring an armed conflict to a successful conclusion quickly and with authority. Armed forces, law enforcement agencies and armed citizens from around the world recognize this and so equip themselves. Up until a few years ago, the shotgun was my go-to gun for home defense.

I kept a short-barreled Remington 870 with a magazine extension loaded with six rounds of No. 4 buckshot under the bed. All through college, I lived in a single-wide manufactured home and found, after some real-world testing in an abandoned house, that 00 buck would shoot completely through a wall and then some. Much to my roommate's relief, No. 4 would just ruffle up the sheetrock's exterior on the far wall.

More real-world testing on feral hogs and various varmints convinced me that both 00 and No. 4 buckshot were near instantaneous fight stoppers out to 25 yards.

A few years into college, I managed to save up enough money to buy a dedicated SureFire 618LS forend and a SpeedFeed stock. It was my attempt to create a Scattergun Technologies model that was absolutely unattainable at the time.

A sweet-shooting AR carbine lends itself to more practice, and that increased level of familiarity will come into play during a high-stress fight.

These two aftermarket additions elevated my gun's performance. Endless slug-select drills allowed me to swap ammunition in mere seconds and extend the gun's range out to 75 yards with cheap, Foster-type slugs. The house gun soon became a truck gun, a welcome addition that sat wedged between the seat and console.

I knew enough then to realize that every nighttime fight would benefit from a bright white light. You could see, identify and shoot a target without having to worry about confusing a crook with a roommate's psycho ex (who found the extra key and was stealthily sneaking in for a late-night visit).

The SureFire's momentary-"On" switch is much easier than trying to hold a flashlight and the forend with the same hand while activating the tail-cap switch and keeping both the light and gun pointed in the same direction. With SureFire's forend system, you also know the light will always be with the gun and not in the truck or at your friend's house (where you left it after looking for her stupid cat).

Relative to other guns, practice costs were not too outrageous. I worked steel over with birdshot loads once a month and impressed friends with my rapidity of fire. Despite moving a dozen times and falling in love with other guns, the shotgun was always there, under the bed or in the truck and ready to defend my home and hide. That Model 870 was one of the few constants in my life, and wherever it rested was home.

CONVERT

My thinking has changed a little on the subject of long guns for home-defense. But the shift away from scatterguns to AR carbines was very gradual. My first AR experiences were with Colt HBARs and standard-pattern rifles with full-length barrels and round handguards. One rifle mounted a variable scope over the carry handle that was awkward and uncomfortable to use. These rifles taught me that iron sights were capable of an amazing degree of precision when properly used. At the time, I thought the platform and caliber were limited to target and prairie dog shooting.

As the incremental progression of rifle and accessory development occurred, so did the AR's applicability in roles traditionally reserved for CQB weapons like short shotguns and submachine guns. Rails allowed us to attach smaller, brighter and better lights to the rifle before improved stocks and vertical fore-grips soon after appeared. Better parts improved reliability.

The biggest advance occurred with the wide acceptance of reflex sights and new shooting techniques that utilized a both-eyes-open approach for faster target acquisition. The rifle's large aperture is quick, but an EOTech, Trijicon or Aimpoint has proven faster and much more precise.

The driving force behind this exponential development was the expanded role of the M4 with military elite and LE agencies. Since their lessons are learned the hard way, the tip of the spear tends to dictate what the rest of the spear wants to shoot. If a system is good enough for the U.S. Army's Delta and the U.S. Navy SEALs, surely it should be my weapon of choice, should I be a police officer or Mr. John Q. Public looking to defend my home.

Intrigued by hazy green images from the front of helmet-clad figures ripping through houses and caves, I bought a Rock River Arms LAR-15 flattop carbine and decked it out with a Vltor Modstock, Aimpoint CompML2 sight and Samson STAR-C rail. It eats ammo so fast I could go broke trying to feed it. Paper, pigs, steel and coyotes all met the little carbine's business end with very satisfactory results. These military guys are on to something. Attaching a light to the forend, I ripped through a darkened shoot house one night and never touched my handgun. It was an epiphany—a properly dressed carbine is a versatile—dare I say "the ultimate"—offensive and defensive firearm. It delivers precise, devastating power at unmatched speed.

GENDER RELATED

Early on, a few range dates with my soon-to-be wife sealed the deal. If she was going to hang out at my place, she damn sure better be able to hold her own should danger come knocking at the door. We drilled with a shotgun several times, and her range debut was impressive (as

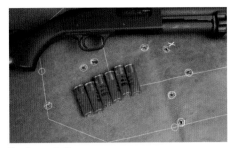

There is no arguing the efficacy of nine .33-caliber pellets at close range. This 25-yard target demonstrates the cylinder bore's pattern at range.

was the bruised shoulder and goose egg on her cheek the following day). She could shoot the shotgun well, but there wasn't much that was pleasant about it.

On our honeymoon to Montana, my wife and I were shooting prairie dogs with a bolt rifle. I broke out my Rock River for grins, picked off a few that were close in and then wailed on a distant rock. My wife asked to shoot the rifle, and two magazines later she had the barrel hot. No recoil and the ability to strike distant targets amount to a lot. We would hit the range to practice with our carry guns, and she ended up shooting the M4 more and more, commenting how much better she liked it over the shotgun.

DEFENSE CHARACTERISTICS

Home defense is an entirely different matter with much more serious consequences. What advantages could a carbine have over the shotgun in this arena? The adjustable length of pull affords shooters of an aftermarket stock a strong consideration for an AR as a "house gun" (should a smaller-statured occupant be called upon to hold the fort). Having watched a dozen youths learn the art of shooting in the last few decades, I think a rifle that fits is the number-one consideration that leads to positive results. My neighbor's kids were able to shoot the M4 better than my adult-proportioned .22-caliber rifle simply because I could collapse the stock enough that they could properly address the carbine.

Recoil is also an important consideration. It increases time between shots by fractions of a second, but more important, it increases time between practice sessions. Even with low-recoil loads, the average shotgun will produce anywhere from 20 to 30 ft-lbs of recoil, while the .223 might squeak out four ft-lbs in a really light gun with a heavy bullet. Leaning into a shotgun, I can get off two aimed shots per

Defensive carbines should be fed lightweight, frangible bullets, not military ball ammo, to reduce overpenetration. At close ranges, the rounds are devastating.

Though on-board ammo capacity is not always an issue in a home defense situation, it is always nice to have more. The AR gets the edge, with 28 or 29 rounds in a magazine. Most shotguns only carry six or nine rounds in a magazine and four or five spares in a stock or side-saddle magazine.

second—my wife, one. With the Rock River, three center-mass shots a second at seven yards are easy. My wife shoots wonderful controlled pairs at the rate of two shots per second.

No one is going to worry about recoil in a life-and-death situation, but even a quick practice session with full-power ammo can push inexperienced shooters past their limits. Realistically, the novice should drill with a home-defense arm at least once a month—dry-fire practice, loading and malfunction drills, shooting from cover, etc.—and send rounds downrange every other month, maybe more depending on the person. Anything less is probably asking for trouble.

Even though the AR's manual of arms is slightly more complicated, the pure fact that one is more likely to practice with an AR because it is much more comfortable to shoot overcomes the additional degree of difficulty. Put an AR and a hard-kicking shotgun in front of shooters of any experience level and ask them to choose. They will most likely pick up the AR (and he who shoots more, shoots better).

MAKE OR BREAK
Ammunition is the make-or-break factor, and improvements in .223 Rem. and 5.56x45mm NATO—more specifically, bullets—are what allows the AR platform to effectively challenge the shotgun. We have all heard the vociferous complaints from soldiers about bullet performance or lack thereof in the Sandbox. For once, the military lessons learned are not applicable to civilians and law enforcement. We are not limited to full-metal-jacket bullets or ammunition produced under government contract.

Instead of going heavy like the military, I prefer lighter, frangible varmint bullets

in the 45- to 60-grain range. The old adage "speed kills" rings true on more than just the highway. Having planted a fair number of varmints and game animals with ARs and .223-caliber rifles, I can readily attest to the cartridge's efficacy. In fact, a .223 loaded with Hornady's 55-grain TAP is my favorite deer-culling cartridge. Head and neck shots are the rule, but quite often body shots are required. I have taken deer from 30 to 300 yards with this combo and found it to be more than adequate. Results at contact or across-the-room ranges would be horrific.

With 55-grain TAP, Hornady's ordnance-gelatin testing reveals that at 30 feet, the bullet penetrates an average of 8¾ inches and has an average retained weight of 17 grains when fired from a standard 16-inch carbine barrel. I usually get a complete pass-through on broadside shots on whitetail deer averaging 90 to 120 pounds at any range.

The retained weight average of just 17 grains would probably get most shooters scratching their heads, most having placed an absolute premium on retained weight. Keep in mind that I have no intentions of shooting through an elephant or through my house and into a car. The bullet will hopefully dump most of its energy in the oncoming assailant and send small fragments of jacket and core out past the main wound channel to do their nasty work before ending up lodged between two layers of wallboard. Inside a house or in any urban environments, frangible ammunition makes for a good choice.

You can hardly get these facts out of your mouth when up comes the argument of barrier penetration, and no, a light bullet moving fast does not penetrate barriers very well. But buckshot or No. 4 shot doesn't defeat barriers very well either, which was the point of using both in the first place.

Some other small points to consider are weight—both guns, when fitted with a light, will be pretty close. My go-to AR all decked out weighs nine pounds, 10 ounces with a 30-

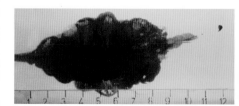

Lightly constructed bullets provide an immediate, incapacitating energy dump and, in most cases, will not overpenetrate.

An AR is much easier to shoot from tight concealment than a pump-action shotgun.

round magazine in place. The pump shotgun with forend light with six rounds in the magazine checks in at nine pounds, 11 ounces. With a standard 16-inch barrel, the AR is four to six inches shorter than the shotgun, depending on stock position. You could shorten both with the right paperwork, which affects the shotgun's capacity but not the AR's.

Should an intruder enter the house, 28 rounds in a rifle and another PMAG stuck in your back pocket is a comforting thought. Topping off from a side-saddle or SpeedFeed stock works well enough, but you have access to four or five rounds at the most and need to practice accessing them. Living in a rural area, the 5.56 NATO obviously has a flatter trajectory than a shotgun slug and easily travels beyond the rifled shotgun's 150-yard max-effective range.

Both guns come into action equally fast. I keep the shotgun's magazine loaded, chamber empty and safety on. Similarly, I keep a loaded magazine snapped into an AR's receiver with the chamber empty. Both require chambering a round (a sound often described as a "Georgia burglar alarm") and disengaging the safety to make them live.

FOR AND AGAINST
Honestly, the AR is no more complicated than the pump gun in terms of fire controls if the shooter practices at all. I think the AR handles a little better, especially when shot from cover. Most range sessions are conducted while standing on the hind feet—a huge mistake. Try working a pump gun flat on your back or from really tight cover. The same goes for weak-hand and one-hand shooting. The AR is easier to manipulate and fire.

Maintenance is no contest. I clean my shotgun once a year, unless it gets rained on, paying particular attention to the magazine tube. The AR is meticulously cleaned and lubricated after every range session, a drawback for some, while other weird individuals find cleaning a rifle mildly therapeutic.

Poor maintenance on any firearm will lead to malfunctions, and the AR is exponentially more likely to jam. I can clear most AR jams in five to seven seconds, but shotgun jams are usually catastrophic in nature. Should either go south in a fight, it's time to transition to a pistol until the fight comes to an end. Remember, two is one and one is none (always carry a pistol even when armed with two of the best self-defense guns).

As in most firearm discussions, there are few absolute truths and the matter usually boils down to personal preference and confidence. Either gun in the hands of an untrained or unmotivated person is virtually worthless, but both guns are capable tools in the right hands. The military and LE veterans training at Academi have turned the scattergun into an instrument of high art, using just the shotgun pattern's edge to snuff out hostage-holding tangos and ringing steel at 200 yards. And my wife is no slouch with her AR. The instructors shoot daily. She shoots every other month, and for her the carbine is a better fit.

Both guns have advantages and disadvantages that must be carefully considered. But the next time some gun-shop commando makes the declarative statement—and they are fond of declarative statements—that the shotgun is the world's ultimate home defense arm, give pause. There's room on the throne for two.

PROTECT

AND SERVE

BY RICHARD NANCE
PHOTOS BY ALFREDO RICO

WHEN I ATTENDED SWAT SCHOOL IN 2003, I had very little

experience with the AR-15 platform. At that time, my police department's issued long gun was a Remington 870 shotgun. After a crash course in shooting, fieldstripping and maintenance of my issued surplus, Vietnam-era M16, I headed out to attend a two-week basic SWAT course, which was all that stood in the way of me becoming one of the newest members of my department's team.

At the range, I was eager to prove to myself and the instructors that, despite my minimal experience, I could handle an AR like a pro. Unfortunately, my rifle didn't cooperate. In fact, it malfunctioned after every round or two. This resulted in me becoming very proficient with the malfunction clearance drill being taught, which consisted of yelling for fellow officers to cover me while I took a knee and fixed the problem.

Somehow, I made it through the day with that long-toothed rifle. The next morning, the SWAT team leader brought me a replacement, which, although dated, functioned properly. During SWAT school, I gained a new appreciation for the AR platform, and, in my opinion, the pistol-caliber submachine guns that so many of the other students had carried were no match.

COLT'S M4 COMMANDO

In 2005, thanks to a government grant, our 15-man SWAT team was outfitted with brand-new Colt M4 Commandos. I had the privilege of greeting these M4 Commandos when they were delivered to our armory. One by one, I removed them from the packaging and began to equip them to the team's specifications.

Colt firearms have a well-earned reputation for quality and reliability, and the Commando is no exception. The M4 Commando is shorter, lighter and more maneuverable than its M16 predecessors. With a barrel length of just 11½ inches, an overall length of only 27.1 inches (stock collapsed) and weighing a mere 5.38 pounds, the Commando was designed to dominate in CQB environments where obstacles, teammates and adversaries can make it difficult to employ a full-size rifle.

The Commando may fall in the lightweight division, but with its 5.56 NATO chambering, it packs the same ballistic punch and close-range accuracy as bulkier, less wieldy tactical rifles. Because of its unique blend of maneuverability and firepower, the Commando has become the carbine of choice for many elite military and law enforcement units. In so doing, the Commando has stolen much of the pistol-caliber submachine gun's thunder.

Our team selected the R0933 model, which features a flattop upper receiver and detachable carry handle. The R0933 Commando can be fired in either semiautomatic or automatic fire modes with a quick 180-degree flip of the right-hand selector.

When you consider that, unlike a traditional battlefield, a SWAT environment will likely contain nontargets in close proximity to, or even held hostage by, suspects who pose a deadly threat, the need for accurate fire is clear. While there may certainly be a time when automatic fire is advantageous, the vast majority of SWAT teams default to semiautomatic fire due to its increased controllability. SWAT operators are responsible for every round fired, even on auto.

Like all Colt rifles, the M4 Commando's upper and lower receivers are made from forged 7075-T6 aircraft-grade aluminum. The lower receiver boasts a four-position adjustable buttstock, allowing the shooter to customize the length of pull. This is a beneficial feature for rifles that are shared, as well as for rifles used with both a patrol-type ballistic vest and much bulkier SWAT body armor.

The Commando's upper features a forward assist as a backup for the rare occasion when the bolt fails to lock into place. The cartridge-case deflector performs its job whether shooting right- or left-handed. The dustcover helps

keep the bolt and chamber free of debris.

The Commando's handguards are lightweight and comfortable, with ample but not ridiculous amounts of space on the top and bottom that can be used to add Picatinny rails.

The Commando is equipped with an A2-style front sight base and an A2 compensator, which minimizes flash and dust signatures.

PERSONALIZATION

Without question, one of the greatest advantages to the AR platform is its modular design. Many times, a user has to reconfigure a rifle to best suit the needs of an operation. In recent years, the "more is better" approach has led to a perversion of the AR's modularity. It seems that some have to use every inch of Picatinny rail space available. Oftentimes, this added weight is detrimental to handling and overall performance.

If you're going to be carrying a rifle for extended periods, a minimalistic approach probably makes more sense. When an M4 is going to be a SWAT operator's primary weapon system, there are two must-have features: a powerful, intuitive white light and a fast, accurate sighting system.

My M4 Commando is equipped with a Sure-Fire M900A vertical foregrip weapon light, which is attached to the bottom of the forend with a section of Picatinny rail. The M900A's

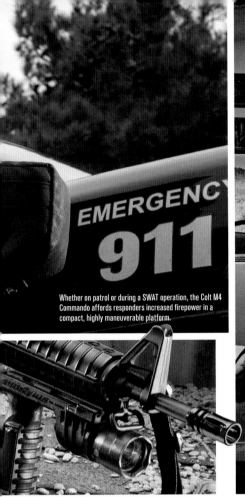

Whether on patrol or during a SWAT operation, the Colt M4 Commando affords responders increased firepower in a compact, highly maneuverable platform.

The four-position, collapsible stock enables the operator to adjust for length of pull. Accessories like the SureFire M900A vertical foregrip weapon light and EOTech model 512 holographic sight make the Colt M4 Commando a very formidable carbine for law enforcement.
Photos by Alfredo Rico

A rapid and accurate sighting system is an integral component of a SWAT carbine. Nothing fills this bill better than a red dot sight, which greatly simplifies the aiming process by allowing the shooter to simply overlay the reticle onto the target, as opposed to trying to align front and rear sights, while focused on the threat.

Our team opted for the EOTech model 512 Holographic Weapons System, which is powered by two AA batteries. The EOTech is mounted to the Picatinny rail, where the optional carry handle once sat. Windage and elevation adjustments are located at the 3 o'clock position and can easily be turned with a coin. The reticle features a 65-MOA circle with one-MOA aiming. The EOTech is durable, waterproof and sports a large window for a wide field of view. The internal optics are fogproof, and the optical surfaces are coated with an anti-glare material.

In the high-stress world of SWAT calls, the point-and-shoot simplicity of an EOTech is hard to beat. At CQB distances, the EOTech affords the tactical operator an unfair but much welcomed advantage.

The only problem I've encountered with the EOTech was that after several years of use, the connections in the battery compartment failed, rendering the unit inoperable. I called EOTech and quickly received several replacement connections that can be installed in minutes without the use of any tools. In a jiffy, my EOTech was back up and running.

Since a SWAT operator has to be prepared for a worst-case scenario, there has to be redundancy to the carbine's sighting system. If the EOTech were to fail during a close-range firefight, the operator could likely deliver combat-effective hits by simply looking through the window of the inoperable unit. However, when time allows, simply flipping up a rear back-up iron sight (BUIS) affords the shooter the ability to aim more precisely.

Our team's Commandos are each outfitted with a GG&G Multiple Aperture Device (MAD)

incandescent light output is perfectly suited for CQB applications. There are pressure pads at the 3 o'clock and 9 o'clock positions, which allow the operator to precisely control the duration of light output. Since lights tend to attract bullets, it's wise to use them judiciously.

In addition to the white light, the M900A is equipped with blue LED navigation lights, which can be used when covert movement is required or even to alert team members to your location in darkened environments. The navigation lights are activated by a pressure pad above the pistol grip that is easily accessible to your thumb. The weatherproof M900A is constructed of aerospace aluminum and impact-resistant polymer. Like the carbine it's mounted to, the M900A is both rugged and reliable.

Photos by Alfredo Rico

The Commando is well balanced, light recoiling and fast in transitioning from target to target. As its name implies, the Commando was designed for CQB. The vast majority of training I've done with the Commando has been at distances from 25 yards to arm's length, with an emphasis on SWAT-related principles such as shooting on the move, in tandem, at multiple targets and from atypical positions. But I was curious to know what type of accuracy to expect from the Commando at farther distances. I decided to shoot the M4 from prone at the 50-yard line and from the 100-yard line using both the EOTech and iron sights.

From a prone position at the 50, I fired five five-shot groups using duty ammo, Hornady TAP 55-grain. With the EOTech's reticle brightness dialed down, I put rounds

BUIS. The MAD sight comes with an integral Picatinny rail mount. It can be adjusted for windage using a dial located at the 3 o'clock position. When needed, the operator can simply flip up the sight.

The MAD sight offers a large aperture designed for CQB, as well as a small aperture to be used when a more refined sight picture is required. The operator can select the appropriate aperture by turning the dial, which protrudes beyond the base of the sight, in either direction.

With practice, the MAD sight can easily be employed even with a gloved hand. A detent located at the 9 o'clock position must be depressed in order to fold down the MAD sight.

I replaced the stock front sight with an XS 24/7 tritium-stripe front sight. This sight contains a tritium insert for low-light conditions surrounded by a white oval that's quick to acquire during normal lighting conditions. I have always been a fan of XS sights. While they may not be the most precise sights on the market, they offer lightning-fast target acquisition, with plenty of accuracy for CQB.

RANGE DAYS

It's hard to dispute the reliability of the Commando. Over the years, the only times I've been able to get it to malfunction (and I've tried valiantly in training) have been when the bolt group was bone dry from hours of mostly auto fire. I take care of this rifle, and in short, as long as the Commando is wet, it will perform.

Just how much should you lubricate the bolt group? At Colt Armorer School I asked that very question of the instructor. His response was, "Imagine dunking the entire bolt group into a bucket of Mobil One synthetic motor oil, then shaking it off a couple times before reassembling the rifle." That's pretty wet.

The XS 24/7 tritium stripe front sight is easy to acquire, regardless of lighting conditions. The Colt M4 Commando is shorter and lighter than its M16 predecessors, with better ballistic capability than pistol-caliber submachine guns, making it perfectly suited for CQB work.

The GG&G MAD BUIS can easily be flipped up should the Carbine's primary sighting system fail. The large aperture is intended for CQB, while the small aperture provides a more refined sight picture for shooting at distance or when accuracy is paramount.

Colt M4 Commando

TYPE	Direct-impingement, select-fire automatic
CALIBER	5.56 NATO
BARREL	11.5 in., cold hammer forged, chrome lined, 1:7 twist
OVERALL LENGTH	27.1 in. (collapsed), 30.4 in. (extended)
WEIGHT	5.38 lbs.
HANDGUARD	Colt M4 carbine
STOCK	Colt M4 carbine, 4-position, collapsible
GRIP	A2
SELECTOR	Three-position
TRIGGER	Mil-Spec
MAGAZINE	Colt, 30 rds.
MUZZLE DEVICE	A2 compensator
SIGHTS	GG&G MAD BUIS
MSRP	$1,706 (LEO)
MANUFACTURER	Colt Defense, LLC 800-241-2485 colt.com

downrange. The tightest group was just over an inch and a half, and the widest was just over three inches, with the average being a hair over two inches. My five-shot iron sight group was a shade under three inches.

After warming up at 50 yards, I hiked back to the 100. Again I fired five five-shot groups of Hornady TAP using the EOTech to aim. This time, I used a range bag and a rear bag rest to stabilize the Commando. The results were surprising, with my best group being just a hair wider than my best group from the 50-yard line. My worst group from the 100-yard line measured just over 3¼ inches. Interestingly, my average group size from the 100 was just less than two inches. Unfortunately, my iron sight group left much to be desired, measuring a whopping five inches.

I tried to comprehend how it was possible for me to shoot better from twice as far from my target. It's certainly possible that I concentrated a little more from the 100 than I did from the 50. Maybe the carbine was better braced at the 100? Another possibility was that, due to the size of the reticle of the EOTech relative to the target, I had a different point of aim. From the 50-yard line I placed the red dot over the orange X-ring of my target. But from the 100-yard line, I placed the red circle that surrounds the dot over the outer portion of the target, which may have been an easier point of reference.

STANDING BY

After eight years, my Colt M4 Commando has become my baseline for comparing ARs. It is by far the most comfortable carbine for me to shoot. Everything is right where it needs to be. I know that with the stock collapsed, extending it one position affords me a perfect shoulder mount when in full SWAT kit. For patrol, it's two positions from collapsed to achieve the ideal shoulder mount.

A rifle's sling is often compared to a handgun's holster. Therefore, it must be both functional and comfortable. Several months ago, I tested and evaluated a VTAC two-point sling, which has since replaced the one-point bungee-type sling I carried for years. The VTAC sling is surprisingly versatile and enables me to keep the Commando steadier when shoulder mounted. For me, this translates to increased accuracy—always a plus when lives are on the line.

I've also developed a slight preference for Magpul PMAGs, which function flawlessly and seem to provide a better gripping surface than standard G.I.-type magazines that came

from Colt. In my experience, PMAGs are less susceptible to being damaged if dropped during a reload.

Whether for SWAT or patrol, my Colt M4 Commando is my go-to rifle when I anticipate armed resistance. I've spent years with the M4, and when you're with something that long, its performance is predictable. The Colt M4 has seemingly become an extension of my body. Should I go into harm's way, it's this carbine I'll have with me.

10 TIDBITS ABOUT MY COMMANDO

1 The EOTech is zeroed at 50 yards.

2 While the tactical latch on the charging handle makes it much easier to cycle the bolt, it can interfere with obtaining a sight picture while wearing a gas mask.

3 The iron sights and EOTech reticle are co-witnessed.

4 On patrol, my Commando is carried in the trunk because the vertical foregrip weapon light prevents it from fitting in the mount designed for patrol rifles.

5 My Commando is stored in a soft case with a magazine seated "chambersafe," i.e., chamber blocking device inserted, and bolt forward, with the selector switch on Safe.

6 The "Gapper" plug fills the void between the bottom of the triggerguard and the top of the pistol grip, making prolonged carry much more comfortable.

7 The XS 24/7 tritium stripe front sight can only be adjusted in full 360-degree increments to ensure that the tritium insert faces the shooter.

8 Turning down the brightness of the reticle enables you to obtain a more refined sight picture with the EOTech.

9 The trigger pull is approximately 6½ pounds.

10 The SureFire M900A vertical foregrip weapon light adds 1.3 pounds to the carbine.

With the EOTech reticle dimmed for more precise aiming, the Colt M4 Commando proved up to the task, even from 100 yards out.

Performance

Hornady TAP Urban 55 gr.	
50 Yards	**100 Yards**
EOTech	
1.59	1.66
Iron Sights	
2.99	5.02
Velocity (fps)	
2,737	

Accuracy results reflect best five-shot group with EOTech and a single five-shot group with iron sights. Velocity results were the average of five shots fired through an Oehler Model 35P chronograph.

STANDING

YOUR GROUND

by KYLE LAMB

AGGRESSIVE AND OFFENSIVE FIGHTING STANCE VS. SHOOTING STANCE.

Top left: Two officers correctly assume the aggressive fighting stance, ready to move or shoot. Top right: Starting movement by simply lifting the front foot off of the ground. Bottom left: Continuing movement from the fighting stance. Bottom right: Continuation of movement. Above: In this shooting stance, neither officer is ready to move efficiently.

Left: Approaching a stairwell, this shooting stance doesn't have the power to fight or move. Right: In this aggressive shooting stance, the officer is ready to fight and move.

WITH THE ELBOW DOWN, YOU ARE PRESENTING A SMALLER SILHOUETTE, ESPECIALLY WHEN CLEARING AROUND CORNERS

It is the middle of the night in some Godforsaken country, and you can smell the stench of the local populace as you make entry into the enemy's lair.

As you cross the threshold into the first room, he is there, caught slightly off guard by the flash-bang device that has just detonated. You know what you must do. You quickly twist your body in such a way that your hard armor is square to the threat. Now you must wait to see if he will hit you in the plate. You have trained for years to be square to the target in order to present a better target for the threat…

Does this make sense? Absolutely not. Why would we train to be shot instead of train to move as quickly as possible, mount our carbine, bring sights on target, deactivate the rifle's safety and eliminate the threat?

SHOOTING STANCE

As I have traveled around the country and various other parts of the world, I have been exposed to numerous interesting shooting techniques, from the cup-and-saucer pistol techniques of some European commandos to the full-auto, spray-and-pray room-clearance techniques encountered on the Dark Continent.

One technique that surprises me is the carbine and submachine gun squared shooting stance. Actually, the technique is not as surprising as the reasoning behind it. When its users are asked why they employ it, they never fail to reply, "I want to present square armor plates to the bad guy." You have got to be kidding. You are going into a situation that will call for you to eliminate another person and you are prepared to present square plates to the enemy? Are you hoping that their marksmanship skills are polished enough to shoot you in your plates? For the sake of arguing, let's dig into the differences between a shooting stance and a fighting stance with the AR.

I prefer to refer to skills as they apply to my mission. If that mission is shooting, use a shooting stance. If your mission is to fight, use a fighting stance. Ultimately, since our mission as tactical shooters is to deliver bullets to live

Left: This squared shooting stance presents no added benefit in coverage by body armor. Right: This bladed stance illustrates how much exposure you have when engaging a threat target.

This is a proper aggressive stance with the carbine at the ready while moving up a stairwell.

WHERE WOULD YOU PUT YOUR HANDS DURING A FIST FIGHT? TRY PLACING YOUR HANDS IN A SIMILAR POSITION.

tissue, not paper targets, I would classify this as fighting and not merely shooting.

FIGHTING STANCE

The squared stance would not be the preferred stance if you were to fight with just your fists. You would blade your body with the support-side foot closer to your opponent than the strong-side foot. You would also keep your weight forward on the balls of your feet to give you the power and mobility that are needed in a fist fight. You will more than likely also keep your hands offset to allow you to protect yourself as well as throw blows.

This stance is unbelievable for employment of the combat carbine as well. Using the bladed stance gives you additional power to drive the rifle from target to target, as well as the ability to conduct muzzle strikes if necessary. There isn't a need to shift weight to start movement forward. Simply lift the front weighted foot, and gravity will take over. You will move much more efficiently.

If the bladed stance is coupled with a support-hand-forward position, you will also have the strength to control recoil better than more aft hand-position techniques. Once again, we want the power to control the fight. This also applies to firearm retention. You will be more powerful with the hands apart than if they were close together on the carbine.

AGGRESSIVE AND OFFENSIVE

When teaching these techniques, we add a few more specifics to enable the shooters to be aggressive, dynamic and offensive.

Weight on the balls of your feet. If you are standing flat-footed, the rifle's recoil will push you back on your heels. You would not want to be on your heels in a fist fight, so why would you with a rifle? Placing your weight on the balls of your feet will not make a big difference if you plan to fire two rounds and stop, but if you plan to shoot until the threat is eliminated, you might want to lean into it. You never know, it may take two, three or 10 rounds to eliminate the threat.

Knees slightly bent. It is best to always have a slight bend in your knees, especially the front knee. This bent knee will help you to control recoil, as well as increase the speed at which you can go from a static to a moving position. Bending the knees will prepare you to take an alternate position with less delay than a straight-legged shooting position.

Support hand slightly forward. Placing the support hand forward will enhance any shooting position that requires muzzle control during multiple shots, as well as increase speed when engaging multiple targets.

This flat-footed shooting stance (left) is slower to launch from. Stay aggressive (right) and be prepared to move.

THE KNEES WILL PREPARE YOU TO TAKE AN ALTERNATE POSITION WITH LESS DELAY THAN A STRAIGHT-LEGGED SHOOTING POSITION.

With the front hand forward, you can drive the carbine much better than if you are holding the front of the magazine well. This technique will also put your hand where it is needed to engage your light system.

Elbow down. With the elbow down, you are presenting a smaller silhouette, especially when clearing around corners. Putting up the chicken wing will give the threat something to shoot at well before your muzzle finds its way around a corner. Keeping the elbow down in a cocked position will also prepare you for any needed elbow strikes in a "no room to shoot, no time to shoot" situation.

Use optimal stock length. Black nylon, Velcro and short stocks are all the trend these days. Actually, I believe Multi Cam is overtaking black at a pretty good pace, but Velcro is still hanging in there. Short stocks do seem Gucci as far as overall length of your battle rifle is concerned, but a short stock is not conducive to being fast, aggressive or accurate. As you pull the rifle closer to your face, you do hit a point of diminishing returns. When the rifle hits you in the face every time you fire, you are too close. You should feel that you have power at all times. Where would you put your hands during a fist fight? Try placing your hands in a similar position during

your next training and see if you can't shoot significantly better. Remember, not all shooting will take place while standing, so try the longer stock in the prone and kneeling positions as well.

Don't crane your neck. If you feel like you are having a hard time getting behind the sights of your AR without putting a lot of pressure on your neck, try sliding the buttstock a bit higher on your shoulder. This will allow you to have a more heads-up fighting stance, increase peripheral vision and allow quicker target-to-target movement.

Think offensive and be aggressive. Next time you start to train with your carbine, focus on a more aggressive shooting stance. Push the limits until that stance becomes a fighting stance. When you get ready to deploy that rifle system, get into an offensive mindset, which is a must if you plan to close with and destroy your enemy.

I have never looked back during an After Action Review and said, "I wish I would have been less aggressive and had a more defensive mindset." From the streets of Mogadishu, Somalia, to Mosul, Iraq, these aggressive fighting techniques have helped us to weather the storm in the Global War on Terror.

The low recoil, low report and high capacity of the Rock River LAR-9 makes it an ideal choice for inside-walls home defense.

UNLAWFUL ENTRY

I admit it. At first I thought an AR-15 in a pistol caliber was as useless as stilts on a flamingo.

Not that I'm opposed to pistol-caliber carbines—quite the opposite. I grew up shooting a reproduction of one of the originals of the breed, a Navy Arms iron-frame Henry in .44-40 caliber. I worked cattle with it slung on my saddle, shot mule deer with it and killed beeves come butchering time in

November. A good pistol-caliber carbine is a very useful tool.

But why, I reasoned, have an AR—even a nice, compact M4-type platform—in a caliber that doesn't compare to its native .223 chambering? A pistol cartridge such as the 9mm is, even when fired out of a carbine, a 100-yard proposition at best, while the .223 is comfortably a 300-plus-yard cartridge. Furthermore, no real capacity advantage is gained. And even though some still call the .223 a "mouse cartridge," the 9mm is even less powerful. Moreover, the receiver is bigger and bulkier than other firearms chambering pistol-caliber cartridges.

I've been wrong before, and a lengthy range session with the Rock River LAR-9 proved I was again. The first thing that struck me was the low—in fact, very low—recoil and

---

SOMETIMES EVEN THE MOST DEARLY HELD OPINIONS ARE WRONG.

BY JOSEPH VON BENEDIKT
PHOTOS BY MIKE ANSCHUETZ

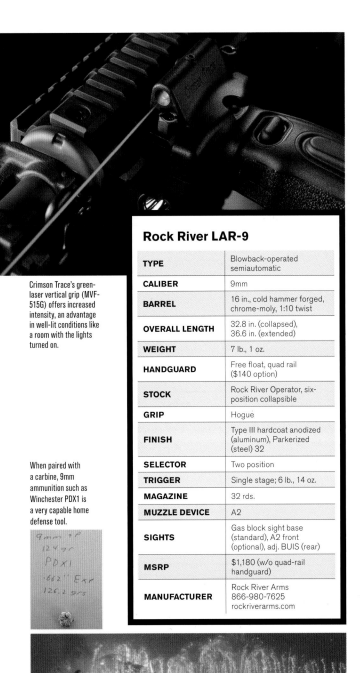

Crimson Trace's green-laser vertical grip (MVF-515G) offers increased intensity, an advantage in well-lit conditions like a room with the lights turned on.

When paired with a carbine, 9mm ammunition such as Winchester PDX1 is a very capable home defense tool.

9mm +P
124 gr
PDX1
.662" Exp
126.2 grs

Rock River LAR-9

TYPE	Blowback-operated semiautomatic
CALIBER	9mm
BARREL	16 in., cold hammer forged, chrome-moly, 1:10 twist
OVERALL LENGTH	32.8 in. (collapsed), 36.6 in. (extended)
WEIGHT	7 lb., 1 oz.
HANDGUARD	Free float, quad rail ($140 option)
STOCK	Rock River Operator, six-position collapsible
GRIP	Hogue
FINISH	Type III hardcoat anodized (aluminum), Parkerized (steel) 32
SELECTOR	Two position
TRIGGER	Single stage; 6 lb., 14 oz.
MAGAZINE	32 rds.
MUZZLE DEVICE	A2
SIGHTS	Gas block sight base (standard), A2 front (optional), adj. BUIS (rear)
MSRP	$1,180 (w/o quad-rail handguard)
MANUFACTURER	Rock River Arms 866-980-7625 rockriverarms.com

report. Compared with the .38 Special and .45 ACP handguns going off next to me at the range, the LAR-9 sounded more like a .22 Magnum. That could prove to be a very real benefit if it's fired within the confines of one's home without hearing protection. We all hope we're never put in that situation, but if we are, I'm highly skeptical that an intruder will pause to allow my family to insert earplugs before shooting.

Though the .223 cartridge typically chambered in AR-type rifles generates little recoil, it creates a lot of muzzle blast, especially in the shorter-barreled versions. And much as we like to think otherwise, recoil and blast do make it difficult to shoot well under stress. The old argument that "you won't even feel it when the moment comes" is a bunch of balderdash. Both recoil and blast can create bad habits during practice, and if you think those bad habits will magically disappear if this critical moment arrives, you're sadly mistaken.

Rock River's LAR-9 is a handy carbine built from the ground up for 9mm Luger. It's completely reliable with the factory-supplied 32-round magazine. The author mounted Leupold's illuminated Mark 4 CR/T topped with the motion-activated Leupold Deltapoint for range testing and a Crimson Trace green-laser/LED light vertical grip.

Considering the attributes of the .223 cartridge, I had to confess that in reality, no self-defense situation we would likely ever meet in society as we know it will require the .223's distance-shooting abilities. The average citizen just doesn't get in Hathcock-like sniper

contests. Citizens rarely get in shooting conflicts that call for a distance-capable cartridge, therefore, the lower noise and the carrying abilities of 9mm Rock River are truthfully an advantage.

The second attribute of the LAR-9 that struck me was the lack of parts on the bolt. There's no such thing as a bolt carrier. The bolt is basically a solid hunk of steel shaped roughly like an AR-15's standard bolt and carrier assembly. The only moving parts are the extractor and firing pin. Even the ejector is a piece of nonmoving steel affixed to the lower receiver. No bolt locking lugs, no rotating bolt head, no gas rings, no carrier, just a chunk of blowback-operated simplicity. Liken it to a massive incarnation of your favorite Ruger 10/22.

Similarly, at the rear of the barrel there is just a polished bevel, no bolt head recess with locking lugs to collect fouling and no gas tube. And since it is a blowback-operated system, there is no gas port to bleed mechanism-functioning fuel from the barrel, no need for the presence of a gas block (though there is a block simply to supply a front sight) and no gas tube inside the quad rail.

The LAR-9 avoids completely the argument between gas-driven impingement systems and piston systems. It needs neither and thus has none of the disadvantages so

Though Rock River builds its own 32-round magazines (right) for the LAR-9, Colt 9mm magazines may be used. Modified UZI mags such as the one pictured here at left may be used as well, though the UZI mag will not hold open the bolt after the last round is fired.

hotly debated—no dirty gas blowing into the receiver, no carrier tilt.

The simplicity of the system impressed me greatly. I did initially wonder if the blowback design would be forgiving when fed a broad variety of bullet weights, and I resolved to prove it out with a menagerie of loads topped with projectiles ranging from 115-grainers to subsonic 147-grain versions. I did so, and the only result was a range littered with cases with no malfunctions whatsoever.

There is something vaguely charming about a stick magazine containing 32 rounds of double-stacked 9mm ammo. It doesn't quite have the panache of a stick mag for the legendary .45 ACP Thompson, but still, one can't help but smile when gripping it and slamming it home.

It can be rather a wrestle to do so on a closed bolt, and leaving a cartridge or two out of the mag doesn't seem to help much. I'm not saying it can't be done, but one must insert it with conviction to be successful. It's much easier to insert a magazine with the bolt locked open. Thankfully, the bolt does lock open on an empty mag and stays locked as that magazine is dropped and a replacement is inserted.

On the flip side, the magazine itself is not hard to load. In fact, putting all 32 rounds in it is easier than loading one of the 15- to 19-round magazines of several of today's popular polymer pistols.

Wondering whether the LAR-9 magazine is proprietary to Rock River Arms, I called the company and spoke with BJ,

Performance

	Black Hills JHP 115 gr.	Black Hills JHP 147 gr.	Hornady TAP 147 gr.	Winchester PDX1 124 gr.	Winchester PDX1 147 gr.	Winchester White Box FMJ 124 gr.
Velocity (fps)						
	1,482	1,054	1,068	1,360	1,044	1,184
Standard Deviation						
	19	25	22	9	7	14
Extreme Spread (fps)						
	46	56	52	18	18	37
100-Yard Accuracy (in.)						
	1.77	2.11	2.22	1.94	1.90	5.10

Accuracy is the average of three five-shot groups fired from a Sinclair benchrest. Velocity is the average of five rounds measured 10 feet from the muzzle with a Shooting Chrony chronograph.

a particularly helpful technician who informed me that, while modified UZI magazines work (in fact, the Rock River version is roughly based on the UZI version), they will not hold open the bolt after the last round is fired. Colt 9mm AR magazines also work, and they do hold open the bolt on an empty mag. So if you happen across a used Colt 9mm magazine at the gun show (most likely tagged at eighty or ninety bucks), you can purchase it and voilà! It works. Personally, I'd rather just give Rock River Arms thirty-five bucks for a brand-new magazine.

In order to capture the real accuracy potential of the carbine, I mounted one of Leupold's 1.5-5x20mm Mark 4 MR/T scopes with the illuminated reticle—a great, versatile optic well suited to a tremendous variety of shooting situations—and targeted a series of 50-yard dots with several different loads.

Just to shake things up and see how useful the carbine could really be, I mounted a MVF-515 vertical grip made by Crimson Trace on the LAR-9's mid-length quad-rail handguard. The aforementioned laser is green, which makes it much easier to see in well-lit conditions than a typical red laser. It does have certain drawbacks such as slightly lower extreme temperature tolerances and a greater thirst for batteries, but believe me, it's worth it in order to be able to see that laser in daylight. The unit also features a quite powerful LED white light. When rotated to full power, it puts out an impressive 200 lumens.

After zeroing the laser, I leaned against a post at 25 yards and fired as rapidly as I could bring the green dot back to the center of the target. The resulting group absolutely

These groups were fired from 50 yards and demonstrate that within the caliber's range, the carbine is plenty accurate. The LAR-9 lower receiver is purpose-built for the 9mm magazine. No cheap conversion units at work here.

chewed out the center of the target, leaving a ragged three-inch hole.

Figuring that while the Leupold Mark 4 MR/T optic was great for accuracy testing, something a bit more suitable for in-the-house shooting distances was called for, I removed the top half of the rear scope ring, replaced it with a top half incorporating a base and mounted one of Leupold's Delta-Point optics featuring a 7½-MOA triangle-shaped "dot" that is—applause, please—motion activated. It's the perfect sight for a home-defense arm, as one no longer needs to worry about fumbling to activate a red dot when the alarm sounds in the wee hours of the night. The slightest twitch turns it on, and five full minutes of complete inactivity turns it back off. It's also waterproof and very shock resistant.

An arm destined for defending hearth and home should be well liked and easily manipulated by all adults within the home. In the end, the final judgment of suitability came down to my wife.

She's a shotgun kind of gal and doesn't particularly care for the complicated manual of arms unique to every AR. Pick it up, pump it, and go to protecting is more her style. However, the LAR-9 is light, easy on the ears and much easier on the shoulder than a 12 gauge. It also holds about five times as much ammo as her Remington 870.

I still like my pistol-caliber lever-action carbine, and I'd still choose a standard .223-chambered AR-15 for defensive work outside, but inside those walls, Rock River's LAR-9 beats both of them all hollow.

NOW WHAT?

YOU'VE JUST SHOT AN INTRUDER IN YOUR HOME. NOW WHAT DO YOU DO?

This is a question that should be in the back of the mind of anyone who keeps a gun for defense. I have no law enforcement background, and I, like many, anticipate that those incredibly tense, emotionally fraught moments after a shooting could present real challenges. I recently called a retired police chief—Gary Poynter of Peoria, Illinois—and asked for a simple to-do checklist. What follows are his responses.

First, Chief Poynter emphasized that it's extremely important to know your local laws and when you do and do not have the right to defend yourself with deadly force. A call or visit to the police department is the best way to find out those laws. Actually shooting at another human is a very extreme action, and you simply must be certain that your life is in imminent danger before doing so.

STEP 1: Call 9-1-1. Tell the dispatcher you were attacked in your home, you fired upon the attacker and you need the police and an ambulance. Be truthful, but don't volunteer a lot of information. The dispatcher will ask pertinent questions and walk you through what to do while you're waiting for the police.

STEP 2: Protect the scene. Don't change anything. (One exception is if the attacker is still alive but nonthreatening, you may want to remove any weapons from his reach.) If there are people about, keep them from walking through the scene. Make a point of recollecting why you shot this person. Specifics are important.

STEP 3: Your gun. The dispatcher will likely ask if you are still holding the gun and suggest that you put it somewhere specific such as the kitchen table (assuming the intruder is no longer a threat) in the condition it was in when used. You don't need to clear it; in fact, investigators prefer that you do not. If you've already put the gun somewhere, tell the dispatcher where.

STEP 4: The police. Ask the dispatcher where to meet the police (front door, front yard), and ask the dispatcher to tell the police you're unarmed. At this point you'll want to consider what you're going to say when they arrive. They'll want to know the "five W's" —who, what, where, when and why. If it was a very cut-and-dried case of self-defense, it's your choice to make a statement. However, most legal counsel will suggest that you tell the police two things: that you were afraid for your life and you would like to have your attorney present before discussing the incident further.

STEP 5: What's next? It goes without saying that the police will confiscate your gun as evidence. If it was a straight-up case of self-defense, you should get it back later. Though I assumed you'd better just plan on going to court, Chief Poynter indicated that's not always the case. Again, if it was a clean-cut case of self-defense, you may only need to make a statement and have a discussion with the coroner. Of course, employ the guidance of a good attorney meanwhile.

CAVEATS: If the intruder is still a threat when you get the 9-1-1 dispatcher on the phone, keep your focus on surviving and neutralizing that threat. Also, be aware that the intruder may have an accomplice, so don't let your guard down too early.

Once you are sure there is no more threat, it's your choice to render aid if you desire, but most folks tend to be pretty shaken up after a deadly encounter and don't want to go anywhere near the attacker. In most cases it's best to wait for the ambulance and allow the professionals to administer aid.

UNLAWFUL ENTRY

PART II
HISTORICAL FEATURES

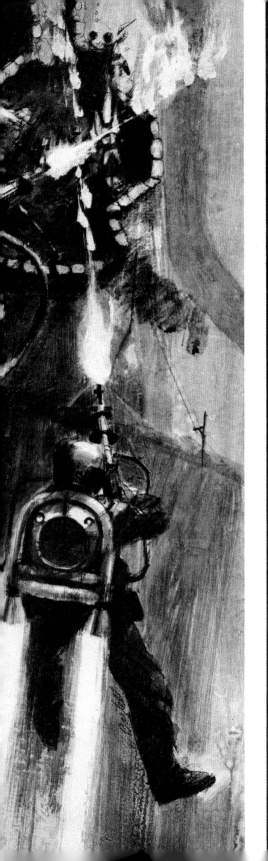

FANTASTIC NEW WEAPONS THAT MAY REPLACE IT!

BY WILLIAM BEECHER
G&A Washington correspondent

Well-designed auto rifles like the AR15 and even space-age super-velocity miniature rockets are the coming thing. As a matter of fact, don't sneer at the thought of a "death ray." It's on the way!

WASHINGTON — A revolution of sorts is raging within the Pentagon. Although highly lethal weapons are involved, no blood has been let. A lot of sniping is taking place, but it's all verbal.

By the time the smoke clears, these results should emerge: devastating new, ultra-modern small arms will replace some present weapons, and tactical doctrine will be rewritten to account for the technological leap forward in weaponry.

At issue are the kinds of individual weapons best suited for modern warfare. Three years ago, when the Army first started equipping the troops with the supposedly up-to-the-minute M-14, the word was circulated that this was the rifle of the future. Today, however, many Pentagon officials — including some top Army, Air Force, Marine and Defense Department leaders —

have completely soured on that weapon.

Some even insist that the Russian AK-47, with which the Red Army and several satellite armies have been armed in recent years, is a better rifle for today's needs, but inferior to our AR-15 or other developmental arms.

Not that the M-14 isn't considered by most military experts an advance over the M-1 Garand of World War II and Korea. It weighs nearly a pound less. It holds a clip of 20 cartridges instead of eight. It fires a 7.62 mm bullet which, theoretically at least, is interchangeable with the ammunition of the other 14 NATO nations.

But one of the M-14's major uses was to be as an automatic rifle; and in that role it has been found badly wanting. In automatic fire it is erratic and hard to handle. Special modifications help, but do not eliminate the basic difficulty.

In fact, while originally the plan was to give each of the ten men in a rifle squad an M-14 which, with the flip of a switch, could be fired a shot at a time or in bursts, now only two men per squad have M-14s set for automatic fire. The rest can be converted only with keys held in limited hands.

The Army devoted 15 years to developing the M-14. Over the last few years it has spent or earmarked over $130 million for 1,390,000 of these rifles (only partly fulfilling its needs) and many hundreds of millions more for ammunition. Despite this tremendous commitment, Army officials have pretty much decided that the future is not for the M-14 after all.

For the time being, the Army is buying 85,000 AR-15s for a large scale test with airborne, air assault and Special Forces troops. The rifle blasts a .223 caliber bullet out at such speed that its velocity smacks a man with "tear-apart" impact.

But, for the future, the Army is looking toward two, possibly three, brand new small arms. All three are heavily cloaked in secrecy. This much, however, can be told:

One of these is a much advanced version of the AR-15. Knowledgeable officials will say only that the weapon has about the same silhouette as the AR-15 and fires the same bullet.

A second highly-regarded weapon is the SPIW (Special Purpose Individual Weapon). It is an over-and-under gun, the lower barrel firing grenades, the upper barrel firing needle-sharp, dart-like bullets at very high velocity.

The most radical innovation of all is the Gyrojet, which strictly speaking is neither a rifle nor a pistol. It fires tiny plastic rockets (that's right, rockets). A cluster of the inexpensive projectiles with their simple tube launchers can be held by one man and fired rapidly at advancing troops. It's said the rockets travel at such speeds that, despite their lightness, they can blow a man apart.

At the present time, high officials are inclined toward either the advanced AR-15 or the SPIW as the next general-purpose infantry rifle. Because of its short effective range, the Gyrojet is thought to be limited to special uses — like jungle warfare.

For many decades the Army prepared soldiers for the ultimate test of combat — the ability to outshoot the enemy — by stressing marksmanship training against fixed bull's-eye targets. But intensive Army research following the Second World War and the Korean

Above Left: Inventor and head of Armalite, Chuck Dorchester, is shown with the three weapons he helped develop. At bottom is the original AR-10. Next is the AR-15 and Dorchester holds the latest addition to the line — the AR-16, which fires the 7.62 NATO cartridge. All three weapons have proved imminently successful and have set the precedent for U. S. military weapons in the near future.

Above Right: Armalite head, Dorchester, gives an amazing demonstration of the versatility of the new AR-16 by firing the weapon with one hand. Note that even the 7.62 NATO cartridge does not give excessive recoil in this particular weapon. The stock folds to the left and merely snaps into place for more accurate shoulder fire. A number of Western allies are interested in this weapon at present.

Editor Tom Siatos fires the AR-15 on full automatic. Note the lack of muzzle rise and no apparent recoil indicated by the fact the photograph is in sharp focus. It is this inherent ability of the AR-15 to concentrate bursts of full automatic fire that give it great potential as a military weapon. Close examination of the photo discloses empty case just clearing the ejection port.

Vietnamese troops, such as this infantryman, are now armed with ultra-modern weapons. This soldier is carrying the AR-15. Light weight, rugged construction and lack of recoil has made it a favorite weapon with these small-statured soldiers in combat.

...is a member of the U. S. Army's special forces stalking a "Fighting Hut" suspected of harboring enemy guerrillas. These special forces are armed with the AR-15 which they have found to be ideal for jungle terrain and conditions in this type of combat.

This veteran of the Army's special forces is shown under actual combat conditions. This is the usual way full automatic weapons are being used in the jungle terrain in Vietnam.

conflict revealed some astonishing and disquieting information: while G.I.s showed they knew how to fire accurately on the target range, in combat only one out of four fired his weapon at all. And of those who did fire toward the enemy, research suggested that in some situations only one shot in 10,000 found its mark.

Of course much firing in combat serves a useful purpose if it immobilizes the enemy by forcing him to burrow deep in his foxhole, allowing our troops to maneuver around his flanks and overrun his position.

Nevertheless the Army became determined to reorient training to see to it that more soldiers in battle would shoot at the enemy and shoot more effectively. A search for a new tack began in 1954 at the headquarters of the U.S. Continental Army Command. In 1957 a whole new approach was launched. Gone were the bull's-eyes. In their place were trainfire courses, utilizing pop-up silhouette targets in combat-simulated settings.

Although the newly-evolving firefight doctrine has not fully firmed up as yet, the trend is unmistakable. We're moving from the take-careful-aim-and-fire approach that dates back to Colonial times, to a point-and-shoot approach. And although logistical problems have in the past limited the number of men armed with automatic weapons, the new look appears to be headed toward a modified automatic fire capability for every man in the squad.

The original concept of the M-14 is one example of this thinking. Another is evident in SPIW development. At first weapons experts experimented with a three-projectile bullet, but dispersion was too great at even short ranges. Now an attempt is being made to engineer the SPIW so that one trigger pull will spit out three separate bullets in quick succession. The effect would be the same as a well-directed burst of fire — hopefully with pretty good groupings at comparatively long distance ranges.

Many technical problems remain to be overcome, but the SPIW is especially well thought of by some officials because it will enable the rifleman to attack both individual soldiers and area targets, like machine gun nests and bunkers. Three manufacturers are scheduled to deliver prototype weapons for initial Army testing next February. The firms, all currently working under modest research and development contracts, are: Aircraft Arma-

ments, Inc., Cockeysville, Md., the Winchester-Western Division of Olin Mathieson Chemical Corp., New Haven, and Harrington & Richardson, Inc., Worcester, Mass. Winchester and H.&R., along with Thompson Ramo Wooldridge Corp. of Cleveland, also make the M-14.

The M-14 grew in large part out of the desire to engineer a versatile rifle firing a cartridge that all NATO nations would use. In the late 1940s, after much argument back and forth, the U.S. and its principal European allies agreed on a standardized 7.62 mm cartridge, actually only a shortened version of the .30 caliber bullet we had been using in our arms since about the turn of the century.

In terms of logistics, this made a lot of sense. For Uncle Sam, the M-14 was to replace four weapons systems — the M-1, the carbine, the Browning automatic rifle (BAR) and the submachine gun — and the separate stocks of ammo required for these weapons. And if all NATO nations used a common cartridge, it was agreed, in any future European war Allied supply problems would be lessened since any NATO nation could use the ammo of any other.

Ironically, although this was one of the principal factors underlying development of the M-14, some U.S. officials assert that certain European manufacturers are making 7.62 mm ammunition with a light charge sufficient to operate some foreign rifles but insufficient to properly operate the recoil system in the M-14.

There is some disagreement on this. In any case the Army now has enough M-14s to fully meet its NATO commitments should a firefight develop in Western Europe. (This means there are enough M-14s to take care of the needs of our five-plus divisions in Europe and our ready-to-move STRAC divisions at home.)

If a decision is made before long to replace the M-14 with an entirely different caliber rifle — as appears likely at present — presumably an attempt will be made to persuade our allies to follow our lead again. There's no telling how hard a fight may be required for this potentially costly move.

In the meantime, the M-14 and its ancestor weapons will continue in the arsenals of our active Army and reserve troops. When about 2,000 U.S. troops were dispatched to Thailand a little over a year ago in a show of force to marauding Red troops in neighboring Laos, the G.I.s carried M-1s. "Not so much because there weren't enough M-14s to equip this relatively small force," says one Army spokesman, "but because we had large stocks of M-1 ammunition out there and very little M-14 ammo." Apparently stocks of M-14 ammunition will, at this time, continue to be built up.

One Pentagon official estimates it may take three to five years before a new general purpose rifle begins to take the place of current small arms. And unless a crash production program is called for, full replacement will take a few additional years after that.

Talk of the possible death of the controversial M-14 has circulated for many months. Last winter when word reached H. & R. that its current order might well be its last, a group of Massachusetts solons called on Defense Secretary McNamara to urge new M-14 contracts for the Worcester company. In the highly influential delegation were Sen. Ted Kennedy, House Speaker McCormack and Sen. Saltonstall, ranking Republican on the Senate Armed Services Committee. Reportedly they were told it was unlikely that new M-14 orders would go to H. & R. but an effort would be made to see what other military contracts the firm might qualify to handle. In February H. & R. received one of the three R & D contracts on the SPIW. Doubtless the firm hopes to share in any large SPIW orders that might eventuate.

For years Army experts have investigated the possibility of using a bullet lighter than the standard .30 caliber. With a lighter bullet, a smaller powder charge can be used, reducing recoil and increasing accuracy. But there has always been argument over whether the smaller caliber has sufficient lethality.

As early as 1928, many Army experts became sold on a smaller bullet. The so-called "Pig Report," so designated because test firings were conducted against pigs, recommended a .225 caliber size. Tests showed the lighter bullet, when properly designed, tended to be unstable and turn end-over-end on entering the target, doing a lot more damage than the more stable, heavier caliber slug.

One Defense official says this recommendation was approved at successive levels of the Army chain of command until it reached the Chief of Staff who spiked it. His name: General Douglas MacArthur.

In 1958 the Army ran a series of tests on the small caliber AR-15, now made by Colt's Patent Firearms Manufactur

ing Co. under license from Fairchild Stratos Corp. While finding some advantages, it still preferred the M-14, especially because of a desire for an effective long-range weapon. Two years later, however, the Air Force said it preferred the AR-15. Some top Marine officers privately took the same position.

Shortly after Defense Secretary McNamara took over in early 1961, a second close look was taken at the comparative merits of the M-14 and the AR-15; the Soviet AK-47 was thrown into the Army-conducted tests for good measure. The results, highly classified, were eye-opening. Generally they showed that while the M-14 at long ranges was the superior weapon, in automatic fire the other two weapons were better, the AR-15 best of all.

The Russian weapon, an adaptation of a German light assault rifle used primarily on the Eastern front in World War II, is considered effective only at very close-up ranges — considerably less than the length of a football field.

The apparent clincher for the AR-15 came in South Vietnam under combat conditions. Tests conducted there by the Advanced Research Projects Agency of the Defense Department showed the AR-15 was outstanding, especially at ranges up to 300 yards. Because of the simplicity and lightness of the weapon and its slight recoil, military men marveled at the ease of training the small Vietnamese troops to use this rifle very effectively.

Pentagon leaders, who put great stress on light equipment, point out that the AR-15 with 120 rounds of ammunition weighs the same as the M-14 empty, about nine pounds. Thus the Army plans to divvy up its 85,000 AR-15 buy among two airborne divisions, one test air assault division and some guerrilla-type Special Forces troops. Army leaders feel this fairly sizeable procurement will provide a thoroughgoing test of the AR-15 and will also create a good production base for the weapon.

And the Air Force, which beat the Army to the draw by previously buying about 27,500 AR-15s, wants to buy another 19,000 this year.

Advocates of the AR-15, and they reside in very high places, insist it is two or three times better than the M-14, that really long ranges are seldom used in combat, and that under mass production the weapon and its auxiliary components will cost 30 to 35 per cent less than the M-14 system (the ammunition will be considerably cheaper).

There are many critics of the AR-15 within Army ranks, too. Some degrade

the weapon as a "varmint rifle," without sufficient range or punch to really compare with the M-14. They charge its light bullet can be too easily deflected by heavy brush and is adversely affected by cold weather.

They agree that new weapons must constantly be under development, but argue that the Army ought to fully meet its mobilization requirements with the M-14 before buying large quantities of other rifles, particularly one some consider inferior.

Without attempting to judge who is right, a reporter may simply note his finding that civilian and military Pentagon leaders who don't want any more M-14s but want instead the AR-15 or some other more advanced automatic fire weapon, seem to far outrank and outnumber those who want to stick with the M-14.

Of course preference for a particular kind of rifle is a rather personal thing to a man whose life may depend on its performance. During the Second World War some infantrymen insisted on using in combat the old bolt-action Springfield rifle or confiscated German weapons instead of the M-1. This was risky in the case of enemy automatic weapons because their characteristic chatter sometimes drew the fire of friendly troops. Nevertheless, Army supply people respected these personal preferences and furnished quantities of the necessary ammo — including captured German issue — to front line outfits in Europe.

Possibly, evolving combat doctrine will in the future make room for one or two sharpshooting snipers per squad, armed with long ranging rifles, perhaps even the M-14.

This article originally ran in the November 1963 issue of Guns & Ammo.

These three cartridges are (l to r); .222 Remington with a 50-grain bullet, .222 Remington Magnum with a 55-grain bullet, and the .223 Remington with a 55-grain full jacketed bullet. While the .222 Magnum and .223 cartridges are similar they are not interchangeable. Both were developed about the same time by different companies each without the knowledge of the other.

A BEAUTIFUL MARRIAGE...
.223 REMINGTON AND COLT'S AR-15 'SPORTER'

Colt has released its "civilianized" AR-15 'Sporter'. Wed to the .223, this combination becomes as modern as tomorrow—a light, accurate pair.

BY BOB HUTTON AND BOB FORKER

Suddenly we find three rifles available for the slowly evolved Remington .223 cartridge.

A cartridge, not quite as large as the .222 Remington Magnum, but with considerably more energy than the more popular .222, has been moved into riflemen's gunracks almost without warning. This is most probably because of the sudden military acceptance. Its military name is 5.56mm but Remington calls its sporting version the .223. All are .224 calibers.

The rifles are the much publicized AR-15 Sporter or Armalite rifle, as now manufactured and marketed by Colt as a semiautomatic (these guns are going on sale at your local dealer while you read this), the Remington 760 slide action, and the third, a strictly GUNS & AMMO target-varmint product made from a Remington 722 action with a new P. O. Ackley heavy barrel and a Fajen varmint stock fitted by Ted Dye. The latter gun, when properly handloaded with target ammo, motivated by Powley Computer, Pressure charts and PMAX, has proved to be so accurate that it will appear this fall in the California bench rest matches in the varmint division. Dale Strawn, chief ballistician for Fred Huntington's RCBS, will be the contestant.

The Remington 760 rifle is not new except in .223 caliber. Special heavy barreled versions of it have been made in .222 Remington calibers for the use of the U.S. Army Marksmanship Training Unit at Fort Benning, Ga. Remington is urging this group to switch to the .223. Remington has also produced this rifle in hunting version and we have completed tests with it.

We have just completed arduous tests with the newly released Colt AR-15 Sporter as well as with a similar rifle in the full automatic version. The AR-15 has been accepted by the military and will be known as the M-16 in 5.56mm caliber. This rifle will be the standard Air Force weapon to replace the M1 Carbine. The Army has contracted for 85,000 of these rifles, with the same number ordered by the Air Force. Remington and Winchester each have received a contract for 59 million rounds of military .223 ammo. Also chambered for the new .223 cartridge in experimental rifles, and not available to the public, are the AR-18, the Stoner 63, the M-16, and the M-16 EL.

In our present tests of the Colt AR-15 and the same gun in military automatic, Burton T. Miller, vice-president of Armalite and for 30 years with the U.S. Air Force, pointed out that military cartridges usually outlive most of their contemporaries. He mentioned the long lived .45-70, the .30-40 Krag and the presumably immortal .30-06 as examples.

In testing the new Colt AR-15 sent us for GUNS & AMMO tests we tried the field stripping instructions provided by the Colt handbook. The AR-15 lesign shows the results of thousands of engineering and development hours. Field stripping is almost as easy as pulling the bolt from an 03-A3. It is started by pushing the take down pin located at the rear of the lower receiver out to the right with the point of a cartridge. You can then pull the pin clear of the upper receiver locking lug with your right hand and break the gun open like a dougle-barrel shotgun. A quick pull on the charging handle moves the bolt carrier group back to the place where you can lift both the bolt carrier and the charging handle free with one hand. That's all there is to it. The critical operating elements of the gun can be inspected and cleaned without difficulty. If necessary, the bolt can be separated from the bolt carrier and the firing pin with a cartridge for a tool. There are no springs in the bolt carrier group, the firing pin being the free-floating type, so there isn't anything to fly apart as you push out the retaining pin. Special cleaning isn't necessary with the AR-15. The usual bore cleaning and action wipe-off is all that's normally needed.

With the school business out of the way we grabbed the ammo and went outside on the range to have fun. Fun we had! The AR-15 Sporter is a real joy to shoot.

The AR-15 follows a trend established by several of the modern military weapons in the use of a pistol type grip for the right hand. The gun is light enough, only 6½ pounds, to be fired from the right hand alone effectively. The very

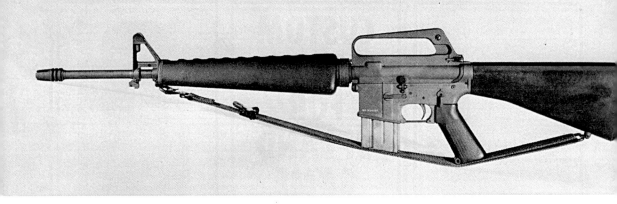

COLT AR-15 SPORTER SPECIFICATIONS

WEIGHT
Rifle without Accessories . . . . .6.3 lbs.
Rifle with Sling and Loaded Magazine . . . . . . .7.0 lbs.

LENGTH
Rifle with Flash Suppressor. . . . . .39 ins.
Barrel . . . . .20 ins.
Barrel with Flash Suppressor . . . . .21 ins.

SIGHT RADIUS . . . . .19.75 in.
Front Sight Post Adjustable for Elevation,
1" click adjustments at 100 yards.

Quick Flip Rear Sight Assembly with Short Range
and Long Range Tangs, Adjustable for Windage,
1" click adjustments at 100 yards.

Effective Sighting Range . . . . .500 yds.

TRIGGER PULL
Maximum . . . . .9.0 lbs.
Minimum . . . . .5.0 lbs.

TYPE OF MECHANISM . . . . .Rotating Bolt
(7 lugs)

METHOD OF FIRE . . . . .Closed Bolt

METHOD OF FEEDING . . . . .5 rounds box mag.

AMMUNITION 223 (5.56MM)
Muzzle Velocity . . . . .Approx. 3100 fps
Muzzle Energy . . . . .1174 Ft. Lbs.
Chamber Pressure . . . . .50/52,000 fps

COST
Suggested retail price $189.50

Guns & Ammo Technical Editor Robert Hutton and Armalite Vice-President Burton Miller (right) discusses some of the features of the new Colt 'Sporter.' The new gun is a sporting version of the AR-15 which was developed by Armalite for the military.

straight stock is comfortable, even for prone shooting. Part of the comfort is due to the sights being raised pretty close to three inches above the center line of the barrel. Still another contribution to shooting comfort is recoil, mild to begin with, and reduced by the operation of the action. The trigger is a real surprise. It is so crisp and smooth that you forget what you are shooting. Compared to the standard Springfield 03-A3 or M-1 Garand triggers, the AR-15 trigger feels like a target rifle.

The sights are also much better than has been the custom on military rifles in the past. The aperture rear sight is adjustable for windage and the post front sight for elevation. In addition, the rear sight has an extra peep for long range shooting. Both front and rear sights have positive notch adjustments that must be moved with a cartridge point. Each notch moves the impact point about one inch at 100 yards. Switching the short range peep to the long range raises the impact point 2.5 minutes of angle. Here's an example of the difference that makes. If the rifle is zeroed at 300 yards with the short range aperture, it will shoot about three inches high at one hundred yards. At 200 yards the shots will be a little over four inches high. If the short range position is used for 400 and 500 yards the drop will be 11½ and 33 inches, but if the long range setting is used with the same sight setting the drop will be only 1½ inches at 400 yards and 20½ inches at 500 yards.

The AR-15 needs its good sights to make use of the accuracy inherent in the gun. The Air Force found that the average group size for AR-15's with 1:12 twist barrels is 2.85 inches at 100 yards. 1:14 twist barrels were reported to be somewhat poorer so the AR-15 is furnished with a 1:12 right hand twist. We didn't have any trouble beating the claimed average performance. Shot from a bench with iron sights in-stead of from the machine rest used for the official accuracy tests, the Colt Sporter consistently produced groups smaller than three inches. Reports to the effect that these guns can't stay on the paper are simply untrue. It's hard to understand how anyone who has fired the rifle could believe this.

We chronographed all three rifles with military loads by Western and Remington as follows: The AR-15 with its 20-inch barrel and necessarily over-sized chamber gave a muzzle velocity of 3250 fps for Western ammo and 3305 for Remington.

In the 722 Remington with the 26-inch Ackley barrel, 14-twist and button rifling, the velocity was 3375 fps with the Western and 3425 for the Remington ammo.

The 760 "trombone"—which incidentally gave fine bench rest accuracy both with hunting and military ammo—had a velocity of 3400 fps with Remington and 3392 with Western.

Our selected test handload in all three rifles was with the 53-grain Sierra boat-tail bullet and 24 grains of IMR 3031. While observing our testing, Miller said this load appeared to perform even better in the action than the military load.

Handloads for the .223 cartridge were tested extensively in the bolt action rifle. This was done before the arrival of the two other arms—the AR-15 and the 760. Loading dies were made to match the .223 chamber, as made by Ackley in the 722, by RCBS. They matched the size precisely, adding to the accuracy produced.

The 50-grain Sierra flatbase bullet with 25.7 grains of IMR 3031 gave 3500 fps and 51,000 psi. The 53-grain Sierra Bench Rest bullet with 25.2 grains of 3031 gave 3440 fps at 51,000 psi. A reduction to 23 grains dropped the pressure to about 46,000 psi and improved accuracy. We obtained even better accuracy with 23 grains of IMR 7122—a Hodgdon powder—which produced just 3000 fps.

With the 55-grain Sierra flatbase bullet, 24 grains of 3031 gave 3320 fps. During these tests the thermometer indicated a temperature of 90 degrees. ◢

The article, "A Beautiful Marriage... .223 Remington and Colt's AR-15 'Sporter,'" originally ran in the October 1964 issue of Guns & Ammo.

Colt's internationally famous AR-15 rifle, known in military circles as the M-16, is the talk of soldiers around the world. The only 5.56mm (.223 caliber) rifle to have been officially adopted by any branch of the U.S. Armed Forces, it is also the only one of these to have been proved in actual combat. South Vietnam's combat zones first welcomed the Colt AR-15 rifle in 1961. Its unique and rakishly efficient straight-line silhouette has since become increasingly familiar to millions, and to the gun enthusiast in particular, through the comprehensive photographic coverage this conflict has received.

Colt's of Hartford, now in its 129th year, is also the only arms company anywhere to have in full production a 5.56mm military rifle. Additionally, the AR-15 is the only military rifle of *any* caliber in production in the United States at this time.

Patent and manufacturing rights on the AR-15 were purchased from the Armalite Division of Fairchild Aircraft, back n 1959. Colt's engineers have since developed two complete weapons systems: the CAR-15 Infantry Weapons System (having a total of 7 configurations, all of them using the AR-15 action), and a compatible machine gun system,

the CMG-1 Machine Gun System (totaling 4 configurations). These combinations have been developed to meet all needs for the modern soldier, and are designed for manufacture at the lowest cost possible (consistent with optimum performance) and with the highest possible parts interchangeability and durability.

The present article briefly reviews Colt's AR-15 rifle, Colt's CAR-15 Infantry Weapons System and CMG-1 Machine Gun System, the accessories to these, and Colt's ultra-modern AR-15 test range. With closed circuit target monitors, water-based bullet traps, and automatic safety devices, the indoor M-16 range is considered a *ne plus ultra* in military target-accuracy test facilites.

With the military designation M-16, Colt's rifle is under procurement as the standard shoulder weapon of the United States Air Force. The first U.S.A.F. contract was awarded Colt's in 1962, and Air Force contracts now total 80,000 rifles. The U.S. Army has contracted for a total of 85,000 AR-15s. Army designation is the XM16E1, and their first contracts were awarded in 1963. The Colt AR-15 rifle is standard issue to Army Special Forces units, to the 82nd and 101st Airborne Divisions, and to other special units

THE COMBAT SOLDIER IS ABOUT TO BECOME AN ELEMENTAL

throughout the world. The U.S. Navy Seal Teams are exclusively armed with the AR-15 rifle. And it is under purchase by over 50 foreign governments throughout the free world for use in combat or tests.

Such an extensive validation of performance has given this light, small caliber, selective fire, straight-line construction weapon a reputation as probably the most famous military rifle of modern times.

Such kudos are, however, nothing new to Colt's Firearms, the Connecticut arms-makers founded in 1836 by the legendary Colonel. Colt's, Inc., is one of five divisions of Colt Industries, a major industrial corporation specializing in miltary defense systems. The firm's experence in military weapons and its readiness to react to the needs of U.S. military forces have been instrumental in the development of the Colt Infantry Weapons and Machine Gun Systems.

All elements of the CAR-15 Infantry Weapons System and the CMG-1 Machine Gun System fire the 5.56mm cartridge, the now widely accepted military cartridge with many features of economic and logistic significance. Light in weight, yet devastating in performance, it literally pokes holes through cinder block walls, and pierces body armor

The concept of the AR-15 is to provide firepower with a low weight factor. The rifles have already been used by our special forces in Vietnam with a high success factor.
U.S. Army Photograph

ARMY WITH COLT'S NEW . . .

AR-15

Above: One of the more unique new features of the AR-15 system is the heavy machine-gun pod. The unit delivers belted 5.56mm rounds to the gun, then collects the clips. Left: The complete AR-15 weapons system is shown as a group. From left to right they are: M-16 (Colt's AR-15) with 75mm grenade; carbine; survival pack gun; submachine gun; heavy assault rifle; grenade launcher (bottom).

Part two of three. Infantry footsoldiers weapons currently under consideration by the armed services. Next month . . . The Stoner 63 system

WEAPONS SYSTEM

FIREPOWER IS THE BYWORD OF MODERN COMBAT! MOBILITY AND ADAPTATION ARE THE BROTHERS OF FIREPOWER! THIS NEW .22 CALIBER ARMS SYSTEM IS INTERCHANGEABLE, LIGHT AND LETHAL, PROVIDING THE INDIVIDUAL FOOT SOLDIER WITH MAXIMUM FIGHTING PUNCH!

AR-15 WEAPONS SYSTEM

or both sides of a steel helmet at 500 yards. Rumors of Russian development of a .223 rifle and cartridge are convincing testimonals to their respective merits.

Though detailed lethality data are not generally available, reports of the 5.56 mm's hydrostatic effects as graphically shown in Vietnam action by the AR-15 rifle offer combat proof of effectiveness that is nothing less than stunning.

Six of the AR-15's major points with heavy bearing to Armed Forces personnel are as follows:

LIGHTWEIGHT

The lockup (rotating) bolt eliminates need for the heavier receiver normally required to support breech pressures in conventional weapons.

The simplified gas operating mechanism reduces weight. Aluminum alloys and plastics achieve lightness and rust resistance, certainly important factors.

Logistically speaking, 440 extra rounds of ammunition can be carried without increasing the weight of the normal field pack.

GAS OPERATING SYSTEM

Bolt and carrier together form a piston and cylinder, which are actuated by the gas fed back through the gas tube, from the gas port near nozzle.

The system eliminates the high maintenance prone operating rod used in conventional gas piston and bolt systems.

STRAIGHT-LINE CONSTRUCTION

The light recoil of the .223 and the recoil's straight back path make vertical dispersion or barrel climb insignificant. This feature has particular military significance in accurate fire on full automatic.

OPERATIONAL SIMPLICITY

Initial charging (charging handle is at top rear of frame), bolt release (center of left side of frame), selector lever (left side of frame, above grip) are designed for fingertip operation. The thumb-operated selector is for safety and for semiautomatic and full automatic fire.

There are no outside moving parts to distract the shooter when rifle is in operation.

Trigger guard adapts to winter operations with gloves by opening through use of a cartridge point.

Sight adjustments (windage and elevation) are likewise by cartridge point.

MAINTENANCE

Permanent lubrication of reciprocating parts reduces maintenance requirements.

One live 5.56mm round serves as the only tool required for routine maintenance and field disassembly to the point of replacing the firing pin. The firing pin itself serves for even further servicing.

Dust cover protects working parts from foreign matter when rifle is not in use, and opens automatically upon firing or charging of the weapon, or releasing the bolt.

Corrosion resistant materials require a minimum amount of care.

Designed with wearability in mind, parts breakage is rare. An A.F. armorer in 1963, on return to the U.S. from Vietnam, answered a question on which replacement parts the AR-15 needed, by stating he didn't know, since "We haven't broken anything yet."

TRAINING TIME

Has been considerably reduced by significant factors which make the AR-15 and the derivatives in the CAR-15 Weapons System easy to shoot. Three of these major elements are: 1, reduced recoil; 2, lack of external moving parts during firing; 3, simplicity of maintenance and operation.

Grenade launcher attachment gives foot soldier an intermediate range weapon to fill the gap between rifle grenades and mortars.

Above: Every AR-15 to reach a combat soldier's hands has been tested in Colt's TV controlled testing range in New Haven.

Right: Authorities have found that trainees become familiar with AR-15 faster than a heavier recoiling combat weapon.

Left: Colt's has recently brought out a scope sight for the AR-15. Look for a *Guns & Ammo* test of this optical innovation soon!

THE WEAPONS SYSTEMS

Under the direction of Colt's Engineering Vice President, Walt Hutchins, the CAR-15 Infantry Weapons System was developed "to meet the point and area requirements of modern warfare." From the basic AR-15 action, Colt's now has available this variety of alternate configurations in answer to the current infantry weapons requirements of all types of ground and airborne forces.

The CMG-1 Machine Gun System complements the Infantry Weapons System for ground forces and provides lightweight weapons for a variety of airborne applications. In order to effect logistic economies, the weapons in this system utilize the same 5.56 mm military cartridge as the AR-15. The light weight of weapons and cartridge allows a significant increase in the number of rounds carried for any given combat load.

These two small caliber, high velocity systems are offered by Colt's as "a substantial step forward in providing increased firepower to the foot soldier and airborne units and as a significant reduction in total weight without sacrifice of reliability and lethality."

AR-15 RIFLE

The AR-15 (M-16) rifle is a gas operated (closed bolt), air-cooled, magazine-fed (20 or 30 round), semiautomatic or fully automatic shoulder weapon. Major physical characteristics of the AR-15 are:

AR-15 Rifle

Weight: Empty, 6.3 lbs; loaded, 7.0 lbs.
Overall length: 39.0"
Barrel length: 20.0"
Note: All barrels in both weapons systems have button rifling, of one twist in 12"
Cyclic rate: 700-900 rounds per minute
Velocity at muzzle: 3250 feet per second
Energy at muzzle: 1285 foot-pounds

CAR-15 CARBINE

The carbine was designed for use by small unit infantry leaders. Colt's shortened the barrel on the basic rifle by 5" to create a weapon permitting greater freedom of movement, while providing the unit leader with combat effectiveness in his personal weapon. Effective range: 500 yards. Major physical characteristics:

AR15 WEAPONS SYSTEM

CAR-15 Carbine

Weight: Empty, 6.1 lbs.; loaded, 6.8 lbs.
Overall length: 39.0"
Barrel length: 15.0"

Cyclic rate: 700-900 r.p.m.
Velocity at muzzle: 3050 f.p.s.
Energy at muzzle: 1135 ft.-lbs.

CAR-15 Heavy Assault Rifle, M-2

Weight: Empty, 8.2 lbs.; loaded 11.75 lbs.
Overall length: 39.0"
Barrel length: 20.0"

Cyclic rate: 700-900 r.p.m.
Velocity at muzzle: 3250 f.p.s.
Energy at muzzle: 1285 ft.-lbs.

CAR-15 Submachine Gun

Weight: Empty, 5.2 lbs.; loaded, 5.9 lbs.
Overall length: 26.0" (buttstock closed);
Barrel length: 10.0"

Cyclic rate: 700-900 r.p.m.
Velocity at muzzle: 2750 f.p.s.
Energy at muzzle: 925 ft.-lbs.

CAR-15 Survival Rifle

Weight: Empty, 4.7 lbs.; loaded, 5.4 lbs.
Overall length: 29.0"
Barrel length: 10.0"

Cyclic rate: 700-900 r.p.m.
Velocity at muzzle: 2750 f.p.s.
Energy at muzzle: 925 ft.-lbs.

CAR-15 HEAVY ASSAULT RIFLE M-2

The Heavy Assault Rifie M-2 fires either from a 20 or 30 round magazine or link-belt ammunition in varying quantities depending on the tactical situation. In addition to the heavier barrel, it has special openings in upper and lower receivers, a new bolt carrier and slide, and a belt feed mechanism. Firing from either regular magazines or from machine gun belts by the quick switching of parts was designed especially for mobile forces. When linked ammunition is not available, the belt feed device is removed and the gun fed from magazines.

CAR-15 SUBMACHINE GUN

The Submachine Gun is designed for use by leaders of small units and by personnel operating where space limitations are a major consideration, particularly in crew-served situations. Effective sighting range is 300 yards, and the CAR-15 Submachine Gun is intended to replace the .45 caliber pistol, the .45 caliber M-3 "Grease Gun," and (for those units which still have them), the M-1 and M-2 carbines. The basic difference from the AR-15 Rifle is the Shortened (telescoping) buttstock and the stub (10") barrel.

CAR-15 SURVIVAL RIFLE

The Survival Rifle is designed specifically for use by aviation personnel. Wherever possible, all non-functional parts have been removed or redesigned, reducing weight and size appreciably. The Survival Rifle and 80 rounds of ammunition will fit into a standard U.S. Air Force survival seat pack.

CGL-4 40mm GRENADE LAUNCHER ATTACHMENT

The 40mm Grenade Launcher Attachment is designed for use with the weapons system to provide point and area fire capabilities to the grenadier/rifleman. Consisting of a launcher assembly, sight assembly, and front handguard, each can be easily attached and removed. Using 40mm anti-personnel ammunition, the launcher has a range of 394 meters. Exhaustive tests have shown that sighting accuracy exceeds current military specifications and the capabilities of existing weapons.

Accessory equipment for Colt's CAR-15 System are the bayonet, 20 and 30 round magazines, a bipod, rifle grenade launcher, and scope.

The bayonet, M8A1, is of knife-type, and slips over the flash suppressor, locking solidly to a lug which is an integral part of the front sight.

AR15 WEAPONS SYSTEM

20 and 30 round magazines:

These are of aluminum stampings, and weigh as follows:

20 rounds: empty, .18 lbs.; loaded, .75 lbs.
30 rounds: empty, .22 lbs.; loaded, .97 lbs.

Bipod is of aluminum, weight, .5 lbs.

The bipod, of clip-on design, can be attached and removed in an instant, to provide increased stability to the rifle for prone, semi- of full-auto fire.

Rifle Grenade Launcher/Flash Suppressor is standard on every basic rifle, and accommodates Energa and current standard U.S. military rifle grenades without any attachments.

Scope is mounted directly on the carrying handle, and is attachable in seconds without the use of tools. Magnification is 3X; weight, 12 ounces.

Early in 1964, Colt's production facilities were augmented by the construction of the M-16 test range which handles a great many thousands of 5.56 mm shots daily. Each rifle is fired from a machine rest in the main building of the three-structure range complex. Firing tubes connect the buildings, and are more than 300 feet in length.

Before acceptance by Colt's M-16 inspectors, each rifle must be fired 70 times in various accuracy and function tests. These are at 50-yard, 100-yard, and 100-meter targets. Additionally, one out of every 5000 M-16s undergoes an endurance test of 6000 rounds. Testing is at both semi- and full automatic fire, and an individual record card is kept on the performance of each rifle.

Closed circuit TV monitors each test-firing station, displaying a picture of the target on a screen convenient to each inspector and on a master screen for the range chief. Positioning of the targets, which are on spools, is regulated by a photo-electric device.

A pump system furnishes a steady stream of water which acts as the cushion in each bullet trap. Inside the water tanks are wire screen baskets to salvage spent bullets; at the same time, empty brass is carried away by conveyors.

A battery of signal lamps beside each firing station warns shooters of unsafe conditions. As an extra precaution, a loud horn sounds to signal a cease fire and a master safety switch is in the office of the range chief. Electrically-operated interlocks guard the access doors of the target houses. This feature guarantees that no one can enter the target area unless the five steel rifle ports at the firing stations are closed and locked.

Combat-proved as lethal, reliable and effective, on U.S. Government contracts and in full production on an economic basis, and now complemented with the CAR-15 Infantry Weapons and CMG-1 Machine Gun Systems, the international fame of the Colt AR-15 rifle is not difficult to understand.

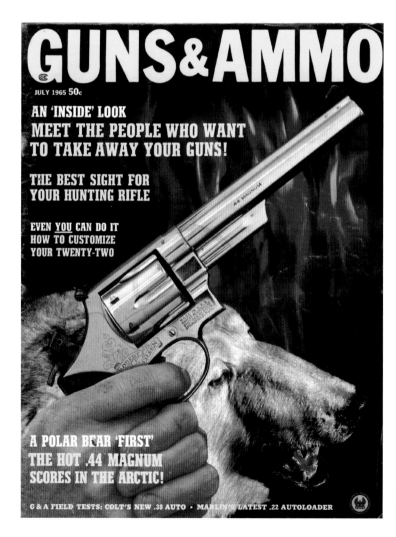

The article, "AR-15 Weapons System," originally ran in the July 1965 issue of Guns & Ammo.

A SPECIAL WASHINGTON REPORT BY BOB NEAL

THE M-16 CONTROVERSY!

Last spring, in one of the bloodiest pitched battles of the Vietnam war, a Marine battalion inched its way to the top of a lonely, battle-scarred knob with the pitifully nondescript name of "Hill 881." • As they fought from slough to hillock, from rock to barren tree trunks, their weapons spewed .223 caliber bullets at rates as high as 850 a minute. But not all of the young Leathernecks were firing. Some were trying to unjam their weapons; some died with their rifles torn down on the dusty ground beside them. • "Believe it or not, do you know what killed most of us? Our own rifles," a young Marine wrote home. "Before we left Okinawa we were all issued the new rifle, the M-16. Practically every one of our dead was found with his rifle torn down next to him where he had been trying to fix it." • And so began another round of controversy for what has become one of the most controversial military small arms procurements in memory. This spring and summer, two separate congressional committees have probed the gun, its mechanical characteristics, the Defense Department's procurement practices and the military's training system. Both sent investigators to Vietnam. • "We couldn't have taken that hill without it (M-16)," the young company commander whose unit climbed Hill 881 has been quoted as saying. • General Wallace M. Greene, Jr., calls it a reliable, hard-hitting, light-weight weapon. But he admits that there has been "some dissatisfaction expressed by a relatively few Marines, but no more than has been experienced in the past when any new weapon has been introduced into our inventory." • Is the M-16 a "dandy or a dud," the New York Times asked editorially, and never quite answered itself. And the answer is not an easy one. Into the answer go the complexities of measuring government procurement policies which have drawn severe congressional criticism — and apparently with good reason. And into the answer, too, feeds the more complex question of the proper weapon for the problem at hand. • Out of a lengthy investigation by Guns & Ammo, statements of field commanders and combat troops, and out of the findings of congressional investigators, the answer appears to be this: • The M-16 is a superior weapon, especially well-suited for the terrain and guerrilla warfare of Vietnam; original models needed modification to match the skills of its users; and the military lost itself in the nightmare of nuclear war and failed to be ready for an escalation of a land war in Asia when it came. • "I'm told that a motto of the Viet Cong is 'beware of units with the black rifle," says Rep. Richard Ichord, D., Mo., Chairman of a House investigating subcommittee. "They've been beset with deadly fear of it." • But General Greene admits there have been problems. "I am not suggesting that there have been no malfunctions or failures," he says. "There are bound to be some." He says some come from an occasional faulty round or a broken part, excessive dirt in the weapon, and, at times, battle stress on the individual firing it. • The new Marine commander in Vietnam, Lt. Gen. Robert Cushman, points up another facet of the controversial M-16: "It is not as

Marine Corporal Richard Jenkins of Mangum, Oklahoma fires the controversial M-16 at Viet Cong during an operation south of Da Nang.
Defense Department Photo (Marine Corps)

The article, "The M-16 Controversy!," originally ran in the November 1967 issue of Guns & Ammo.

M-16 CONTROVERSY

forgiving as some other weapons. It must be cleaned and treated by the book," he says. "No weapon will forgive you if you neglect it."

There are few detractors of the M-16 as a mechanism, but there are some. The problem of jamming is most often cited. Its lack of accuracy at ranges over 300 yards has been criticized, as has its lack of penetration. But most who have fired it, like most combat veterans, come away impressed. Yet its history from a commercial gun to a standard issue combat weapon almost assured that it would be enmeshed in controversy.

The M-16 was the victim of military "vacillation, indecision, stops and starts, delays and changes of policy that have plagued the Army's rifle program since 1945," the Senate Preparedness Investigating Subcommittee charged after reviewing the history of the military small arms modernization program since World War II.

If the gun is a good one (and Lt. Gen. Lewis W. Walt, former Marine commander in Vietnam says it is the "finest weapon the troops have ever had"), then what went wrong? Does it jam, and if so why? Can it stand battle conditions in Southeast Asia?

The M-16 is lightweight, weighing only 6.5 lbs. and is only 38.6 inches in length. It can fire on full automatic as fast as 850 rounds per minute although the average top rate was 750 in earlier models, and since modifications, about 650. It has a muzzle velocity of 3,250 feet per second and fires .223 cal. (5.56 mm.) ammunition, which tumbles when it strikes a target, causing great damage.

The gun was developed by Fairchild-Hiller, and licensed to Colt for production. It was originally developed as a commercial weapon, and named the AR-15.

Colt has done a superb job in manufacturing the rifle strictly according to specifications and with traditionally fine Colt workmanship, as well as meeting delivery dates either right on schedule or in advance. If further studies prove that there is something drastically wrong with the M-16, Colt will have to remain completely blameless.

In the late 1950s the M-14, a heavier (8.97 lb.) automatic weapon firing standard NATO 7.62 mm ammunition with higher accuracy at distances above 300 yards and greater "takedown" power with a single bullet, was adopted as the standard military combat weapon after competitive tests against the AR-15. Planning centered on the need for a long-range weapon for a land-war in Europe and the need for a standard NATO weapon. (The M-14 is still stand-

ard in Europe for U.S. and other NATO troops.)

While the AR-15 was developed privately, the M-14 was developed with some $500,000 in Uncle Sam's money, according to the investigating committees. It was noted that, firing a heavy load, it tended to pull up and away from the target when on automatic.

But in 1962, a highly critical report by the Defense Department Comptroller General reached the Secretary of Defense. It said the AR-15 was up to five times as effective as the M-14, and went so far as to charge that the M-14 appeared to be "somewhat inferior" even to the old M-1. So, a new study was made, and the final conclusion again backed the M-14, charging that the AR-15 "is less reliable, has poor pointing and night firing characteristics, its penetration is marginally satisfactory, and its adoption would violate the NATO agreements."

The Senate committee hints that it was NATO agreements that tell the story. But at any rate, the conflicting reports threw Pentagon gun buyers into a quandary. They finally decided they would continue the M-14 as the standard weapon and buy 85,000 M-16s to outfit special forces. By 1963, they dropped the M-14 from further procurement, and decided to await production in 1969 of the exotic SPIW (for Special Purpose Individual Weapon).

Thus, from some time in 1963 until about December, 1965, small arms orders were nil. Then, with the war in Vietnam escalating and on the demand of General William Westmoreland, for the M-16, the Army asked Colt to produce 25,000 a month.

This is the delay and fluctuating policy that apparently is causing most of the trouble. There were some bugs in the early combat versions of the M-16. In all, according to the House Armed Service Investigating subcommittee, there have been some 40 modifications of the original weapon.

There were some problems with the original issue gun in the field, however, and jamming was one. One reason was discovered to be that standard gun grease could not withstand the temperature and humidity of Vietnam in an automatic weapon firing that fast. It was replaced with a heavier lubricant. There were reportedly shortages of cleaning kits, and this sophisticated gun needs a daily cleaning.

The hiatus in going into full production meant that for a long time, men were being trained in this country with the M-14 then handed the M-16 as they left for Vietnam. They had no real chance to get used to the weapon before going into combat.

In his letter, the unnamed Marine wrote: "Before we left Okinawa we were all issued the new rifle, the M-16." The

Army had less trouble because it was the first to get the weapon, and by the time of the big escalation, its troops headed for Asia were training and living with the M-16. Now, all Army and Marine training of troops for Vietnam get some 30 hours of combat drill on the M-16.

This lack of training probably contributed to the jamming problem. Fighting men, in the heat of battle, are tempted to let their 20-round clips run out at full rate. A gun in combat constantly on automatic is probably more susceptible to a malfunction, the investigators believe.

Last December, the Army and Colt decided to cut down the rate of fire, on the average about 100 to 150 rounds per minute. A spring-loaded buffer was replaced with a series of plastic discs. This reduces heat buildup and slows the speed of moving parts somewhat to cut down wear. Weapons in the field were modified in short order with replacement buffer groups by the troops. Chrome plating the bore to cut down wear and corrosion is being considered, now.

There are other controversies surrounding the M-16. The U.S. State Department gave Colt a permit to sell some 20,000 modified versions to the government in Singapore over an 18-month period. This came as charges were flying that there weren't enough on hand for our own troops. Colt had stepped up its monthly production to 27,500 to produce enough to meet delivery schedules ahead of its annual vacation shutdown this summer. But a union struck the plant, and that further raised the hackles on congressional backs.

A spokesman for the military told *Guns & Ammo* that as of early this summer, the Defense Department could only absorb the 25,000 to 27,500 weapons a month it had ordered from Colt, so the Singapore sale didn't make much difference. The strike, however, could hurt.

Under congressional prodding, the Army purchased the patent rights from the manufacturer on June 30 for $4.5 million and announced it would soon take bids for a second supplier. The second supplier would be in full production within a year, he said. Meanwhile, the Army would set up the distribution, spare parts depots, and other facilities to increase the number of guns it can take from production lines, he said.

In spite of the controversy that has plagued the gun, it appears to be destined to be the standard weapon in Vietnam and similar battle areas for many years. In time, should the rate of attrition slow down, it could become a special purpose weapon in all areas, one military spokesman predicts. While it may have started out to be a one-shot procurement, the total is likely to reach to a million or more.

GI .22

IS THE M16 DEBUG

FINAL JUDGEMENT WILL BE RENDERED BY THE FIGHTING MEN WHO STAKE THEIR LIVES ON ITS RELIABILITY.

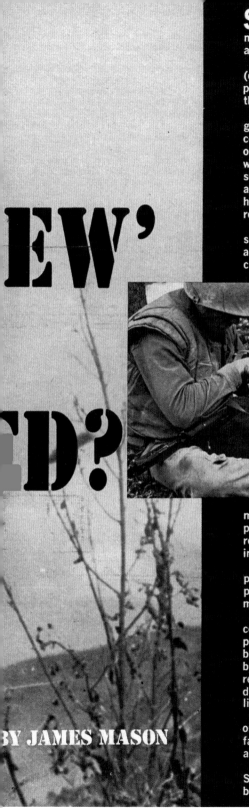

EW'
D?

BY JAMES MASON

So much has already been written about the M16 rifle that too many misconceptions have been created about it in recent months. An objective examination of the M16 is called for to put a finish to doubts and concern.

The report of the Special Committee on the M16 Rifle Program (of the House Armed Services Committee) provides a most complete and accurate register of the circumstances surrounding the whole M16 program.

The report points up findings of the Ichord Committee investigations conducted in the field. A small percentage of Marine combat personnel had definite objections to the M16 rifle based on what they had experienced as unreliable functioning of the weapon. However, the vast majority of troops recognized the superiority of the lightweight M16 over the older M14 rifle for application in Vietnam. These same troops also pointed out however, that the M16 was less forgiving of neglect and required regular, thorough cleaning to keep it in reliable working order.

With any firearm, certain design characteristics create unforeseen operating difficulties. The M16 represents a considerable advance. The uses of aluminum, plastics, and stainless steel create departures from the past complete use of ordnance steels.

The mechanism uses a form of gas actuation not commonly employed; the use of a .22-caliber cartridge for an issue weapon is unprecedented in military ordnance.

All small arms systems are compromises, and the M16 has set departures from traditional arms design that reflect the future. It is an interim weapon design that was first procured because it was available for special applications in the kind of counter-insurgency operations experienced in Vietnam.

The M16 actuating system taps gas from the bore about 15 inches from the breech. This gas pressure is conducted through a stainless steel tube to a chamber inside the bolt carrier, where it expands against the end of the breechblock and the carrier itself. The breechblock remains stationary, while the carrier is forced rearward by the expansion of gas pressure. This movement effects a 20 degree rotation of the breechblock by action of a pin on the bolt following a cam cut in the bolt carrier.

This design eliminates the need for an operating rod and places all moving parts coaxial with bore. Such an arrangement promotes smoothness of operation, especially during full automatic fire.

The unlocking action happens so quickly that there is still considerable remaining or residual pressure (10,000 to 12,000 psi) in the breech following the passage of the bullet from the bore. This transient residual pressure helps operate the action by forcing the empty case out of the chamber and assisting the rearward movement of the breechblock and its carrier. (The dependence on residual pressure allows for the reliable use of lighter weight operating parts.)

The timing of all these reactions is rather critical and depends on constant gas pressure, volume, and relatively stable frictional factors in the mechanism. It is in timing that most malfunctions arise with the M16.

The gas system for the M16 was designed by Mr. Eugene Stoner, and was first employed in the Armalite AR-10 rifle, chambered for the 7.62mm NATO cartridge. It was later adapted to the AR-15 mechanism. The utilization of high-velocity .22-caliber cartridges makes functioning of gas systems more critical due to the drastically reduced gas volume in the bore, and reduced pressure pulse time due to increased projectile velocities.

The AR-15 mechanism was carefully balanced to function with a given standard loading of IMR 4475 powder. This propellant is not significantly different from IMR 3031, except that burning characteristics are rather fast. Pressure curves, therefore, rise more rapidly and peak sharply. Chemical combustion using 4475 was relatively complete before the bullet passed the gas port in the barrel, minimizing the deposit of carbon.

In January of 1964, the Defense Department contracted to have all future lots of 5.56mm ammunition loaded with powders equivalent to WC846, a ball-type powder made by Olin Mathieson Corporation (Winchester-Western) and used to load 7.62mm NATO cartridges.

nificantly the pressure entering the gas system through the gas port.

Increased pulse pressures caused the mechanism to cycle faster. Full automatic rates of fire increased from 850 rounds per minute (certified maximum) upward to 1000 cycles or more.

With increased pulse pressure, unlocking time in a gas system happens faster, all other things being the same. This means residual chamber pressures will also be higher at the moment of unlocking, increasing friction between chamber walls and the cartridge case. Residual gas pressure, which normally gives an assist to operation, now acts as a brake, tending to stick the case to the chamber walls. Meanwhile, the unlocked breechblock is moving to the rear.

Result? At times, a stripped rim, leaving the empty case in the chamber.

dues. A cleaner burning powder might lower probable incidence of stoppage but it most certainly will not eliminate malfunctions from other forms of fouling. On the other hand, diligent care and cleaning of the weapon will reduce all types of stoppage.

The photos show parts of an M16 which was fired more than an average infantryman would in several days of combat. However, even in this dirty condition, this particular weapon functioned normally in all respects. This would seem to uphold the official contention that daily cleaning of the M16 will eliminate 90 percent of its difficulties which are due primarily to neglect, compounded by adverse climatic conditions in Vietnam.

The M16's steel bolt carrier reciprocates inside the aluminum receiver's guideways. Without adequate lubrica-

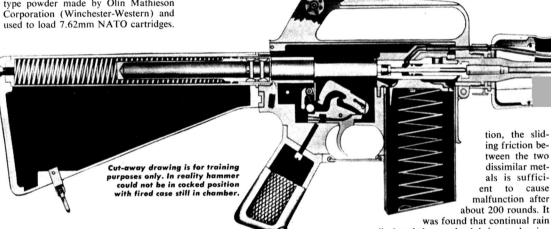

Cut-away drawing is for training purposes only. In reality hammer could not be in cocked position with fired case still in chamber.

tion, the sliding friction between the two dissimilar metals is sufficient to cause malfunction after about 200 rounds. It was found that continual rain displaced the regular lubricants, leaving the bimetal surfaces to gall or seize.

A new lubricant, MIL-L46000A (LSA), has been issued to overcome this problem. The lube holds tenaciously to any surface and is not so easily displaced by water. As long as its coat-

With the prospects for heavy production of 5.56mm ammunition due to the expanding Vietnamese commitment, ball powder was available in quantity at relatively low cost, compared to the IMR extruded propellant. With standardized powder in both 7.62mm and 5.56mm rounds, production facilities would be standardized.

Of major consequence to the reliability of the M16 is the fact that WC846 ball powder burns more slowly, which materially aids meeting velocity and maximum pressure requirements for the high-intensity 5.56mm cartridge. Chamber temperature can be kept down with ball powder, adding to barrel life of the rifle.

However, along with economies and improved ballistic performance, the slower burning WC846 powder also caused increased residues in the bore and gas system. Another adverse characteristic was that the slower burning powder moved the peak pressure curve forward. This is what contributed to improved ballistic performance with ball propellants, but it also raised sig-

This is especially true if the chamber is caked with powder residues, or is etched by corrosion. The rifleman will then have to clear the resulting double-fed cartridge and proceed to use his cleaning rod to ram the stripped-rim case from the chamber.

Furthermore, if residual pressures are unduly high at the time of unlocking, the case head can be stretched enough to cause a separation, leaving the forward portion of the case stuck in the chamber. Since there is no ruptured case extractor presently issued for field use with the M16, the weapon is rendered useless. A ruptured case extractor is under development and may be in the hands of troops as this article is published.

Data from technical investigations show that the vast majority of combat stoppages with the M16 are due to improper cleaning. The fact may be that WC846 powder causes a higher incidence of probable stoppages from resi-

One of the most important engineering changes for the M16 is the new "buffer" or spring guide (top). By increasing inertia on opening stroke it decreases the cyclic rate of fire.

ing is intact, electrolysis between steel and aluminum parts of the M16 is virtually eliminated.

Many GIs tend to over-lubricate a weapon, nearly as detrimental as no lubrication at all. Excess lubricant holds powder residues and foreign matter around tolerances between parts, resulting in increased friction and/or blockages. Proper cleaning and maintenance is the key.

Certain design characteristics of the M16 gas system are relatively conducive to stoppages. However, experience has shown that these stoppages are virtually eliminated by proper cleaning and maintenance of the weapon. The most common malfunctions and their remedies will illustrate:

Excess carbon and pitting in the chamber results from uncleaned carbon build-up, hence increased friction on chamber walls. Condensation entering the chamber forms very mild acids with carbon residues, and rusts and pits chamber walls. Even in a clean chamber, previously scored chamber walls increase friction enough to trouble the more timing-critical .22-caliber gas system. Chromium plating of the chamber to alleviate this condition has been introduced.

Excess carbon under the extrac-

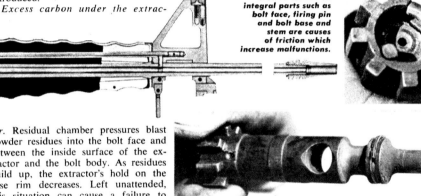

A drop of oil on the change lever shaft keeps the fire control lever from sticking on "safe".

Powder residues, fine brass shavings and crusted carbon on integral parts such as bolt face, firing pin and bolt base and stem are causes of friction which increase malfunctions.

tor. Residual chamber pressures blast powder residues into the bolt face and between the inside surface of the extractor and the bolt body. As residues build up, the extractor's hold on the case rim decreases. Left unattended, this situation can cause a failure to clear, leaving a fired case in the chamber. This extractor problem coupled with the rough chamber and sticking cases mentioned above, can be most deadly. Again, proper maintenance in removing brass and powder residues from the bolt face and extractor lowers the probability of failures markedly.

Dirty ammunition is the cause of many stoppages in combat. The ammunition gets dirty mostly from dust, wind, and mud, perennial problems for infantrymen. In Vietnam, 5.56mm cartridges had been issued in 20-round boxes, resulting in a few loose rounds getting dropped on the ground during magazine loading operations. Recent lots of ammunition have been packed in expendable bandoleers with 10-round strippers to speed magazine reloading and reduce the incidence of dirty rounds.

Damaged or faulty box magazines have always been a problem. Earlier in the war, troops were loading 21 cartridges into 20-round magazines, contributing to faulty feeding of the first few rounds and to weakening or distortion of the feed lips. The taping together of several magazines makes the

The M16 is easily opened and most critical parts are quickly accessible for cleaning. Certain bolt assembly parts do, however, require detail stripping to clean crusted carbon.

M16 DEBUGGED?

lips of the spares vulnerable to damage and dirt. Although it is discouraged in training, a few troops continue to do it.

Loose magazine catches have caused feeding failures. Due to the magazine not being supported high enough in the magazine well, fresh rounds are rammed into the front of the magazine well rather than the chamber. The M16 magazine catch can be easily tightened during maintenance, but redesign could eliminate the problem as well.

Failure to clear (extract and/or eject) has been far and away the most serious malfunction with the M16. There are two types of failure to clear. The first results from insufficient momentum of the bolt carrier to retract far enough to eject the fired case. It may often result from excess carbon or rust in the gas cylinder area and/or in the locking abutments. This increased friction on the bearing surfaces between the bolt and bolt carrier or locking lugs is enough to slow unlocking and use up kinetic energy needed for the full cycling of the mechanism. This is due almost entirely to poor cleaning and maintenance coupled with adverse climatic conditions.

The other failure to clear is more serious and more complex. It involves the leaving of a spent case, or a portion of it, lodged in the chamber. A variety of causes can make this happen. These stoppages seem to derive from marginal operating factors rather than any gross deficiency in M16 design. The nature of this kind of stoppage correlates with early-opening characteristics found occasionally in malfunctioning gas-operated weapons.

The early-opening "syndrome" relates to the use of ball propellant in the M16, with its more intense pulse pressures, elevated cyclic rates, and higher residual chamber pressures. In an unmodified M16 rifle these factors can cause the stripping of the extractor over or through the case rim (leaving the whole case in the chamber), or the rupture and separation of the case. Elevated cyclic rates with the use of ball powder in the M16 are symptomatic of this situation. To overcome the condition, a new, heavier spring guide or "buffer" has been designed to augment inertia during the initial movement of the bolt carrier just prior to unlocking.

The hollow buffer tube is filled with five mild-steel cylinders, separated by neoprene discs that soften accelerations and prevent battering of the steel segments. This added weight increases opening time of the mechanism, giving the higher pulse pressures from the ball propellant more inertia to overcome in the first phase of an operating cycle. The few added ounces of weight mate-

rially lowers the speed of unlocking, allowing chamber pressure to drop to more acceptable levels before unlocking is completed. The camming action of primary extraction then becomes more effective in unsticking the case, eliminating strain on the case rim from the extractor.

An impact-resistant plastic plug in the rear of the new buffer absorbs the shock of moving parts at the end of the recoil stroke, and further slows the cyclic rate. This improvement has lowered rates of fire nominally by 150-200 rounds per minute. This device will probably do more to overcome the functional ills of the M16 using ball powder than any other single mechanical "fix."

Chromium plating of the chamber has been incorporated to reduce friction between chamber walls and cartridge case. It will also protect the chamber from the ravages of corrosion in the damp Vietnamese climate. Accumulation of carbon on the chamber walls should be decreased, since residues will tend to be blown clear of the chamber rather than to adhere to chromed chamber surfaces.

Cartridge case design also has a profound effect on the functioning of automatic weapons. The 5.56mm cartridge fired by the M16 has about the same diameter-to-length ratio as the .30-06 case. Long, thin case proportions create sticking problems at high cyclic rates in automatic weapons. It is a bit late to think about this, needless to say, but a fatter, shorter cartridge case of the same capacity as the .223 Remington round would function in the M16 without nearly so much difficulty. Case sticking and head separations would be reduced considerably by the use of stubby case design. (The chrome-plated chamber will eliminate most of this problem, however, even with the .223 case.) Of course, magazines would have to be made longer to accommodate any given number of stubby cartridges as compared to the present .223 case diameter.

The continued use of ball powder in the M16, or some other powder with essentially the same characteristics, is indicated, since desired ballistic performance cannot be maintained with faster burning powders. The plus factor of ballistic performance from slower burning powder far outweighs the inconvenience of consistent cleaning maintenance by the rifleman. It must be remembered that the M16 would still require regular cleaning for reliable operation even if powder residues were eliminated.

Marine Corps small arms training with the M16 rifle has increased from 10½ hours to 26½ hours for infantry trainees, before they are even assigned to combat units. Integration of the best techniques in field maintenance worked out in Vietnam is being taught by veteran instructors; the effects of early mis-

information about M16 care and cleaning have been overcome.

Brand new M16s are now routinely test fired in conjunction with zeroing and familiarization. Because of close manufacturing tolerances, the weapon's parts do not function smoothly and consistently until after they have fired a few hundred rounds. Some GIs at one time experienced this difficulty, since their weapons had been issued only a

Marine Corps Photo

Lieutenant General Lewis W. Walt, USMC Assistant Commandant of the Marine Corps

In preparation of this article the author interviewed Lieutenant General Lewis W. Walt, USMC, Assistant Commandant of the Marine Corps. At that time he stated, "As the Commanding General of the Third Marine Amphibious Force (III MAF) in 1965, a requirement developed to equip every Marine in my command with a lightweight, hard-hitting automatic weapon. This weapon had to be rugged enough to withstand both the combat and environmental conditions prevalent in Vietnam.

Following the completion of exhaustive environmental tests and evaluations of several U.S. and foreign weapons, the M16A1 rifle was found to be superior. It was adopted for use in Vietnam to meet the requirements imposed by the jungle-type combat enviroment.

As may be expected with any new mass-produced weapon, malfunctions occurred which were immediately investigated and analyzed. Corrective measures were initiated by everyone concerned with the manufacture, test, operation, and maintenance of the weapon and ammunition.

I watched the performance of the M16 in Vietnam closely following its introduction, and discussed the operations and functioning of the weapon with the Marines of my command. The vast majority of the Marines I talked with had nothing but praise for the weapon, including those officers and men who fought in the battle for Hills 881 and 861. A Company Commander who fought in the battle for Hill 881 categorically stated that in his opinion his company was only able to seize the objective because of the M16 rifle.

Reports received during February and March of this year (1968) indicate that the M16 rifle has performed well. In the heavy fighting which has taken place during this period, the malfunction rate has diminished. This trend can be attributed to the efforts, at all levels of command, to improve the performance and reliability of the weapon."

few days before. Coupled with a lack of experience in handling the new weapons, and instances of inadequate supply of cleaning materials, a few experienced malfunctions with the new M16s. Failures were not as widespread as impressions in the press indicated.

Some World War II veterans may recall the change from the 1903 Springfield to the M1 Garand. Marines at Guadalcanal shunned the M1 as being unreliable; " . . . all those moving parts." Their scorn turned to admiration when the superior firepower of the M1 was demonstrated. M1s became the desired combat weapon and many hundred were "liberated" from Army troops sent to relieve the First Marine Division at "The 'Canal."

Put into perspective, the difficulties with the M16 are far outweighed by the other characteristics of the weapon. It is ideally suited to the war in Vietnam, being lightweight, easy to control, and flexible in employment.

The .22-caliber ammunition fired by this weapon is deadly within effective combat ranges, and the lightweight cartridges allow a greater number of rounds to be carried by each rifleman. On the other hand, the light 55-grain .22-caliber bullets are mutilated on contact with heavy jungle cover, thus cutting down the amount of penetration in thick foliage. This situation may be improved in the future by using more durable components in bullet construction.

Barrels of .22 and smaller calibers tend to hold condensation in the bore due to the effects of capillary action and surface tension. If a weapon is fired with even a small amount of water closing the bore, very high chamber pressure is generated. This can be sufficient to cause a malfunction or to blow up the rifle. The water cannot be shaken from the bore, but it will run out of its own accord if the muzzle is depressed and the bolt is opened slightly to break the air pressure seal formed by the cartridge in the breech. Many riflemen use a muzzle cover to avoid accumulation of condensation in the bore during the wet season.

Malfunctions with the M16 have not been widespread; the vast majority of troops have experienced no serious difficulties with the rifle, contrary to newspaper reporting. The public usually hears only the more sensational aspects of a controversy. In reality, M16 failures have been spotty and random but of serious enough proportions to require definite improvements. Thorough technical analysis has shown 90 percent of the malfunctions to be due to improper maintenance of the weapon.

Troops sometimes jokingly talk about the M16 as being made by Mattel Toys, because of its straight plastic stock, aluminum receiver and sights. Aluminum means a lightweight weapon with more ammunition to carry per man. The straight stock and pistol grip means

control in automatic fire, more rounds on the enemy before he can shoot back. The plastic stock means no warpage or swelling in the monsoons; some M14 wooden stocks became so swollen in the Vietnamese climate that the trigger group could not be removed to field-strip the weapon.

At the Marine Corps Base, Camp Pendleton, California, nearly 13,000 troops fired 1.2 million rounds of ball-propellant ammunition through 3950 M16 rifles; there were only 7 malfunctions. Six of these were due to dirty weapons and one failure to feed was caused by a damaged magazine. This performance certainly rivals that of any other individual weapon ever issued to United States Forces.

On the other hand, the little black rifle has had difficulties in Vietnam, where combat conditions evidently have caused some marginal performance. These problems have been dealt with

most effectively by applied maintenance training and major engineering fixes, notably the heavy buffer (to slow down cyclic rate) and chromium plating of the chamber (to reduce friction and protect against corrosion).

In the meantime, evidence overwhelmingly supports the use of the M16 rifle in Vietnam. The Defense Department, after considerable deliberation, is deeply committed to M16 procurement. Field commanders and military professionals praise it; only a very small percent of GIs knock it. Its combat virtues are many; its failings have been few and many have been corrected by the time you read this. It is not the ultimate infantry weapon; indeed, it is a forerunner in the state-of-the-art. The whole situation was summarized by Col. A. L. Emils, G-3 Officer for the Marine Corps Base, Camp Pendleton, when he said: "We have a good weapon. We are looking for an even better one."

The article, "Is the 'New' M16 Debugged?" originally ran in the November 1968 issue of Guns & Ammo.

By PATRICK SWEENEY I Photos by MIKE ANSCHUET

THROWBACK

CENTURY C15A1: EVERYTHING OLD IS NEW AGAIN.

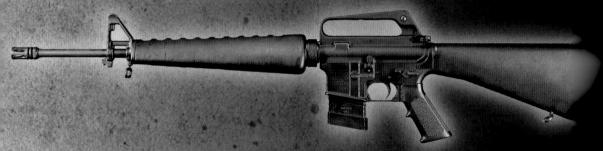

A funny thing happened in the rush to make new, improved AR-15s: The old ones got a lot more respect. While there were people busy trying to wrestle all the "rail estate" they could onto the Stoner platform, some shooters were going back to the future, back to lightweight guns, back to retro.

The original AR-15 (which is what it was before it was the M16 or M4) was meant to be light. As in a carbine that weighed less than six pounds and a rifle that weighed less than 6½ pounds. Compared to those, the modern A2 or M4 clone, at almost eight

The original A1 flash hider is plenty good enough to control muzzle flash, as long as you aren't prone in the desert.

pounds before anything is bolted to it, is an anvil. Some shooters appreciate light weight more than they desire the ability to bolt on a passel of electronics.

But how to get your hands on one of those older ones Well, you could scour parts providers and build one. O pay top dollar for an original. Either approach requires time, effort and the former more than a little gunsmith ing ability. But just when you thought it was going to be hard, you find you can just get one from Century Arms

What Century did was simple. It bought a warehouse full of used M16A1 rifles, scrapped the lower receivers according to the instructions of the ATFE, then rebuil them as semiauto rifles here in the U.S. A change in reg a few years back meant that Century could not import the barrels, and those either stayed behind or were torched here in the U.S. But considering the life that most M16 rifles that had been shipped overseas lead, the barrels were probably pretty tired anyway. I've seen a bunch o the ones that stayed here, and even those can be found with newly made barrels plugged in. In this instance the government has probably done us a favor: You get a brand-new barrel in the bargain. (Let's not encourage them, shall we?)

So, what is this rifle like, and how does it differ from an original? The C15A1 is an A1-uppered (the uppers are original) rifle with a "pencil" barre with a 1:9 twist and an A1 flash hider on the end. The upper has the original forward assist, with the tear-drop button that was replaced by the bullseye button for the A2 models The bolt and carrier are USGI, right out of the M16s with no modifications.

The handguards are the triangular, tapered originals, and they are made (in case you aren't up on your Vietnam-era ordnance) in right and left pairs.

If somewhere down the line you break one, you'll have to order either a set or just that side. They do not switch. However, getting a new pair is not difficult. The slip ring that holds the handguards in place is the period-correct (you'd expect that) flat ring, not the newer, wedge-shaped delta ring.

The rear sight is the A1, with windage adjustments and a long-range setting by flipping up the "L" sight. The front is the original sight tower, removed from the M16A1 barrel and installed on the replacement. The flash hider is A1, and the new parts and old have been given a new black oxide coating.

Inside, the original parts are there. The carrier is an unmolested M16 carrier, marked with the Colt "C" on the side, and the bolt is the same. These are all USGI parts, which also means that you probably have an extractor and spring that are more than

Century Arms purchased a bunch of M16A1 rifles and retrofit them to meet BATFE import regulations. And for the most part, they are all A1. There are some minor differences, including using an A2 pistol grip with a finger hook. For about ten dollars, reproduction A1 grips are available, as are originals, which run about fifty dollars.

30 years old. While the extractor is probably just as good as it was on day one, you might want to upgrade the spring. Going from a standard 1970s spring to a current heavy-duty spring with internal bumper (and perhaps even a De-Fender or Crane SOPMOD o-ring) might be wise.

The lower is a new, semiauto only made for Century and so marked. While it is marked on the left sight, it isn't marked on the right, a point in its favor with the retro crowd. The stock is an A1, which means it is 5/8 inch shorter than an A2 stock, should you have one to compare with it. On

the buttplate is the trap door for a cleaning kit or whatever else you'd care to store there. Internally, the fire control parts have been replaced. While it might have been possible for Century to modify the old parts, it was probably no more costly, and a lot easier, to simply yank them out of each package and replace them with current, semiauto-only parts. And it probably made getting the ATFE to approve the build a lot easier, too. So the hammer is the current notch-top AR hammer, the trigger has the back end of the box closed, and the disconnector and safety

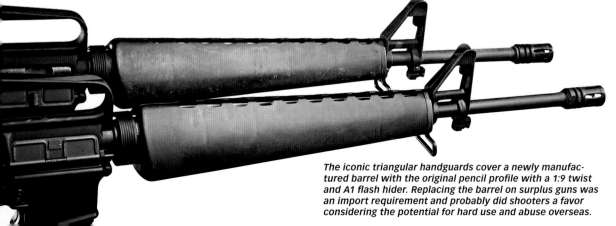

The iconic triangular handguards cover a newly manufactured barrel with the original pencil profile with a 1:9 twist and A1 flash hider. Replacing the barrel on surplus guns was an import requirement and probably did shooters a favor considering the potential for hard use and abuse overseas.

are semiauto-only parts. They're all good ones, and the trigger pull is well within MIL-SPEC standards. The buffer is original, pre-H series, and if you are going to shoot your C15A1 a lot, you might want to keep in the back of your mind the idea of an H or heavier buffer as a replacement.

These are all the good things. There are a few details that the really hardcore retro guys will have some complaints about, so let's get them covered. The first one I heard, and literally scratched my head over, was the magazine. A plastic, 20-round magazine? Like, who cares? If you're a firearms manufacturer and your product needs a magazine to function, you have to include a magazine if you're going to sell a self-loading firearm of any kind, right? Original, or original-pattern, 20-round magazines are not exactly rare. In fact, I even know of warehouses (alas, not for any but the military) full of original 20-round magazines, unused in their boxes. They are everywhere, and cheap. Go out and get all you want. If you aren't looking for period-correct retro magazines, then the job is even easier. There are now plenty of top-notch magazine makers who will sell you all you want for a better-than-fair price.

One big deal is the finish. Current ARs and M16A2/ M4 rifles are done in black. The originals were done in two different shades of gray, and it wasn't uncommon to see mismatched upper and lower rifles in military service before the change to the M16A2. Well, the C15A1 is done in black. And to make sure the new lower and the old upper match, the uppers were dyed (anodizing uses a dye to make them black) to match the new receivers. The hardcore retro guys will grumble, but there is an easy solution: US Anodizing. They know all about the color differences and can match the early or late gray that you desire. All you'll have to do is detail-strip your rifle and send in just the aluminum parts for anodizing. If you want to go whole hog, you can send the relevant steel parts along for phosphating, too.

When the A2 modifications were adopted, the lower receiver went through some changes as well. Primarily, they are on the front and rear assembly pin areas. The front received a

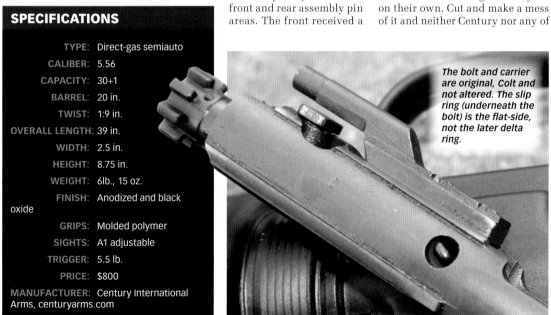

The rifle is supplied with a chintzy plastic magazine, though tons of original, like-new surplus magazines are available.

larger-diameter radius under the bottoms of the front lugs, resulting in more metal there, making it stronger. The rear also received a reinforcement panel, making it larger. Now, most shooters don't care about that. They see the triangular handguards, the A1 sight, they're happy. But the retro cognoscenti want more, and some of them will no doubt go and carve on their lower receivers to remove the offending metal. They do so in the full knowledge that they are on their own. Cut and make a mess of it and neither Century nor any of

The bolt and carrier are original, Colt and not altered. The slip ring (underneath the bolt) is the flat-side, not the later delta ring.

SPECIFICATIONS

TYPE:	Direct-gas semiauto
CALIBER:	5.56
CAPACITY:	30+1
BARREL:	20 in.
TWIST:	1:9 in.
OVERALL LENGTH:	39 in.
WIDTH:	2.5 in.
HEIGHT:	8.75 in.
WEIGHT:	6 lb., 15 oz.
FINISH:	Anodized and black oxide
GRIPS:	Molded polymer
SIGHTS:	A1 adjustable
TRIGGER:	5.5 lb.
PRICE:	$800
MANUFACTURER:	Century International Arms, centuryarms.com

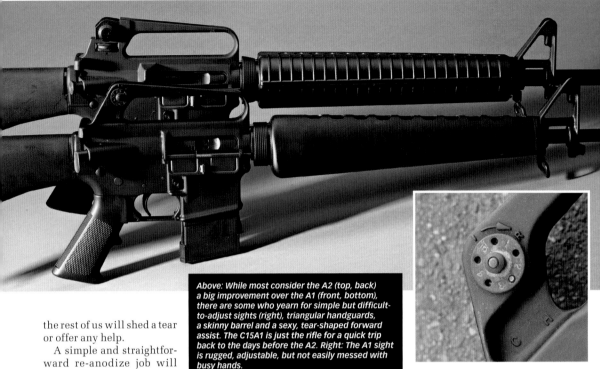

the rest of us will shed a tear or offer any help.

A simple and straightforward re-anodize job will make all but the pickiest shooter happy.

On the two rifles I had to examine, the old front sight towers were attached to the new barrels by different people. While they both were on straight (something you can't take for granted on imported AKs, for example), one of the assemblers was a bit neater than the other. Both were on tight and, as I said, straight, so once I had noted it, I didn't bother fussing over it. If it bothers you, consider this: I've seen honest-to-God USGI M16s that had uglier installations done.

And the last, most minor quibble: the pistol grip. The grips on these are A2 grips, which a lot of shooters like. I didn't notice the difference in the grips much, but it is easy enough to rasp off the finger hook and use some polishing cloth to smooth off the face. Or just hunt down and buy an original (maybe fifty dollars) or a reproduction (ten dollars) A1 pistol grip.

The C15A1 has an original spec'd stock with a length of pull ⅝ inch shorter than the stock found on the A2.

But the real question is, How well does it shoot? Pretty well. Despite the original extractor spring, I had no failures to extract or eject. I didn't thrash the loaners or abuse them, and were I going to hang on to

one of these, I'd certainly upgrade the extractor spring to the current standard. But as-is, they worked just fine. Given the 1:9 barrel twist, I used just the usual assortment of 55-grain and lighter ammo, full metal jacket

The supplied plastic magazine worked fine, and with a day of no caffeine and no wind, the author shot two MOA or so. Not at all bad, and plenty good enough to drop targets.

and JHPs, with one exception: I had a pile of Black Hills ammo on hand loaded with Hornady 60-grain V-Max bullets.

Now, the great joy of retro is the light weight. However, it comes with a price: Getting a scope on your retro is a hassle. One might even say it sucks. In the old days we'd even go so far as to saw off the carry handle and pin, then bolt, epoxy or duct tape (and sometimes all of them) a Weaver rail on top to place a scope. I wasn't going to saw off the carry handle just to mount a scope to check accuracy. Trying to aim consistently with a scope mounted in the carry handle is a fool's quest. Your face moves around so much, any accuracy differences you notice are more likely to be you, not the rifle or ammunition.

So I simply took the rifle (I had sent one of the two back to the studio for photography) with me on a series of range sessions. On one session, when I was in the groove for accurately shooting, I plopped the rifle down into the sandbags and did my best with the existing iron sights. With Black Hills 52-grain JHP match ammo, I was able to consistently shoot two-inch groups. For me, with that trigger, that day, it was quite consistent. And groups like that will make it easy to drop the 300-meter computer pop-ups at the National Guard base.

Ejection was consistent with all loads, and the empties were tossed to the right and behind, as they should be.

If you have been lusting for an early AR, something light and handy, this is just the thing. You could, if you wished, hunt down a similar parts kit, then find your own barrel and lower receiver, and you might (and I emphasize *might*) be able to do it for less money. But if you aren't fully up on building an AR, one mistake will erase your hard-earned discount.

If you want a light, early-features AR, this is just the ticket. And with some searching, you could easily fill out the complete Vietnam-era gear setup: web gear with period-correct ammo pouches, ALICE pack, all the items needed to put your AR right back into 1969.

ACCURACY AND CHRONOGRAPH DATA

Ammunition	Bullet (grs.)	Velocity (fps)	ES	SD	Accuracy (in.)
Hornady	40 TAP Urban	3,267	37.6	12.5	2.5
Hornady	55 TAP Urban	2,950	52.6	22.3	2.0
Black Hills	52 JHP	3,049	75.5	33.1	2.0
Winchester	55 FMJ	3,014	82.3	27.9	3.0
Wolf	62 FMJ	2,812	112	53.1	4.0

Chronograph: PACT MKIV, 18-inch screen spacing, centered 15 feet from the muzzle. Average of five rounds. Accuracy: sandbagged bench rest, 100 yards, average of four five-shot groups.

The great advantage of the AR is the low recoil, with no upward jump. And in a light rifle like the C15A1, packing it all day is not a chore.

Photos by Mike Anschuetz

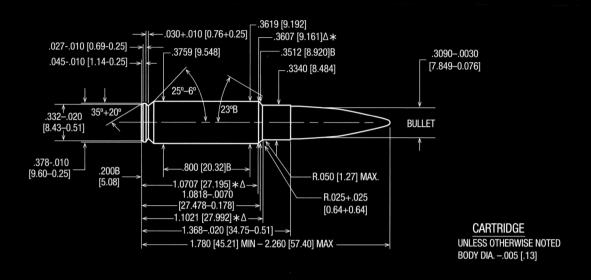

.027-.010 [0.69-0.25]
.045-.010 [1.14-0.25]

.030+.010 [0.76+0.25]
.3759 [9.548]

.3619 [9.192]
.3607 [9.161]Δ*
.3512 [8.920]B
.3340 [8.484]

.3090-.0030
[7.849-0.076]

25°-6°

23°B

35°+20°

.332-.020
[8.43-0.51]

BULLET

.378-.010
[9.60-0.25]

.200B
[5.08]

.800 [20.32]B
1.0707 [27.195]*Δ
1.0818-.0070
[27.478-0.178]
1.1021 [27.992]*Δ
1.368-.020 [34.75-0.51]
1.780 [45.21] MIN - 2.260 [57.40] MAX

R.050 [1.27] MAX.
R.025+.025
[0.64+0.64]

CARTRIDGE
UNLESS OTHERWISE NOTED
BODY DIA. -.005 [.13]

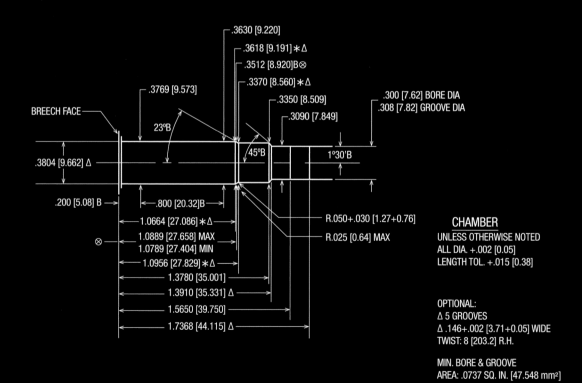

.3630 [9.220]
.3618 [9.191]*Δ
.3512 [8.920]B⊗
.3370 [8.560]*Δ
.3350 [8.509]
.3090 [7.849]

.3769 [9.573]

.300 [7.62] BORE DIA
.308 [7.82] GROOVE DIA

BREECH FACE

23°B

45°B

1°30'B

.3804 [9.662] Δ

.200 [5.08] B
⊗
.800 [20.32]B
1.0664 [27.086]*Δ
1.0889 [27.658] MAX
1.0789 [27.404] MIN
1.0956 [27.829]*Δ
1.3780 [35.001]
1.3910 [35.331] Δ
1.5650 [39.750]
1.7368 [44.115] Δ

R.050+.030 [1.27+0.76]
R.025 [0.64] MAX

CHAMBER
UNLESS OTHERWISE NOTED
ALL DIA. +.002 [0.05]
LENGTH TOL. +.015 [0.38]

OPTIONAL:
Δ 5 GROOVES
Δ .146+.002 [3.71+0.05] WIDE
TWIST: 8 [203.2] R.H.

MIN. BORE & GROOVE
AREA: .0737 SQ. IN. [47.548 mm²]

BY J. GUTHRIE

How respect was earned.

THE

300
Blackout

STORY

There are all kinds of words that could describe a cartridge's development and passage into the shooting world. Circuitous, tortuous, arduous, complicated and convoluted are just a few. Engineers, ballisticians and production managers anguish over every dimension and component, arguing about thousandths of an inch, one or two grains of weight and a hundred pounds this way or that of pressure per square inch. Prototypes are tested, tested again, refined, often rejected, and the slow process goes marching back to square one. The .300 AAC Blackout cartridge is no different and had a long, tough and interesting development path before showing up in military armories and on dealer shelves. Its development story is fascinating.

Almost as interesting as the cartridge itself are the people who worked on the project. Robert Silvers, now the Director of Research & Development for Advanced Armament Corporation, started working with the company back in 2006. While his degrees from the Massachusetts Institute of Technology were in the computer sciences, Silvers always had a keen interest in firearms, ballistics and silencers.

His ground-breaking work and extensive efforts to collect data in the silencer world lead to silencertalk.com, the Blackout flash suppressor and eventually to several silencer designs of his own. Before going to work for AAC full time, Silvers licensed a couple of suppressor designs to the company. In fact, AAC's silencer for the U.S. Army's M2010 sniper rifle was adapted from a Silvers design.

A "U.S. military customer," as Silvers put it, approached AAC in 2009 about developing an improved and modified version of the .300 Whisper. Silvers would not say exactly who the customer was and neither would the half dozen other sources I contacted for this story.

It was the ability to produce a complete package—rifles, suppressors and ammo—that worked which brought the military customer to AAC. As a member of Freedom Group, AAC could leverage relationships with other Freedom Group companies like Remington and Barnes to deliver exactly what the military customer was after.

"They wanted to deliver .30-caliber bullets from an AR-15 at subsonic and supersonic velocities," Silvers said. "They had looked at doing this before with the .300 Whisper, but it didn't work out."

The .300 Whisper, trademarked by the brilliant pioneer ballistician J.D. Jones in 1992, was the most standardized cartridge in a long line of .30-caliber cartridges made from 5.56x45 mm, .223 and .221 Fireball cases. Most of the wildcat cartridges were designed with two ballistic profiles in mind. The first was launching heavy bullets over 200 grains at subsonic velocities. The advantage for special forces operators is the ability to take a short-barreled rifle, suppress it so that it is very quiet and still maintain a high degree of lethality at moderate ranges. The second profile, sending 110- to 125-grain bullets downrange at supersonic velocities, allowed operators to match the AK-47 out to 300 meters with a very compact weapon. Obviously, if the cartridge matched an AK in energy, it would be as lethal and do a good job penetrating intermediate barriers and body armor. Even with tremendous improvements in 5.56 NATO ammo, the new-concept cartridge would be more lethal at engagement ranges from the muzzlebrake out to 300 meters.

"I was interested in the project right off the bat and knew I wanted to do it," Silvers said. "I went to AAC founder Kevin Brittingham, and he was on board and supported it right off the bat. We then went to Remington and, after some discussion, they finally said yes."

Prior to being approached by the military, extensive experimentation with the Whisper and 7.62x39mm had shown Silvers some big shortcomings in the existing .30-caliber ARs.

"I really didn't care about the subsonic rounds at first and concentrated on the 7.62x39," Silvers said. "I tried a bunch of different magazines and just couldn't get any of them to work—there was just too much cartridge taper to run in the AR."

Next Silvers tried a dedicated AR lower that would accept AK-47 magazines. The steel feed lips would hit the bolt carrier and cause issues. Even after machining the bolt carrier, Silvers ran into problems.

"After 300 or so rounds I blew up the bolt and then broke the replacement bolt in another 300 rounds," Silvers said. "You just had to relieve the bolt face too much for it to work. The military was going to need something that would hold up to thousands and thousands of rounds, not 300."

After experimenting with the Russian round and mags, Silvers looked at taking Remington's 6.8mm SPC and modifying it to accept .30-caliber bullets since the case head was smaller than 7.62x39mm. The military took a look, did not like the concept and referred Silvers back to their desire to field something along the lines of the .300 Whisper, mostly because it did not require new magazines that gave up five or six rounds to accommodate a bigger case. But the Whisper had shortcomings too, at least in the eyes of AAC's military customer and Silvers.

"There were essentially three big problems with the Whisper," Silvers said. "The adjustable gas block, reliability and ammo cost."

And from a purely legal standpoint, Remington had a policy against producing any cartridge that had not been approved and spec'd by SAAMI. It was time to start from scratch, sort of. The .30/.221 and Whisper concept was sound, but needed refining. Silvers and the design team had two options, make existing stuff work or take a ground-up approach. To solve all of the problems, they went different routes depending on what would work best for the military customer.

"ARs chambered for .300 Whisper needed an adjustable gas block to go from subsonic to supersonic ammo," Silvers said. "Military guys do not want to mess around with a hot gas block in the dark and if you had the setting wrong it would jam the rifle. Not good. We knew we would have to create subsonic ammo that generated enough gas pressure to run the rifle."

SAAMI MAP pressure for the .300 BLK runs 55,000 psi and at those pressures will push a 110-grain bullet to around 2,300 to 2,400 fps out of a 16-inch barrel. So it is relatively easy to get rifles to run with supersonic ammo. Subsonic loads usually run in the 30,000-psi range, a far cry from supersonic pressures. It is possible to get rifles running reliably at lower pressures by upping the volume of gas in the system. The answer was to use a propellant that produced plenty of volume. Remington's ammo guys were able to crack that code pretty quickly, developing subsonic loads that fooled the rifle into thinking it was running at supersonic pressures. The other key factor in the gas equation was choosing the right operating system for the rifle's barrel length, but more on that later.

Once Remington started producing test ammo on a large scale, thousands of rounds were sent downrange and data recorded for every shot. Remington first used the 123-grain bullet developed for the .30 AR, essentially an AK bullet made to .308 diameter. Several thousand rounds into testing, the data revealed an issue.

"We noticed it was not as reliable as we thought possible," Silvers said. "You could only see it after firing 10,000 rounds, but ammo with an overall length of less than 2.1 inches was statistically less reliable."

Silvers was soon convinced it would take a purpose-built bullet projectile, a longer bullet with the right

radius, to ensure maximum reliability. Remington had thousands of rounds ready to ship, but held off to get the cartridge exactly right.

"The magazine rib rests on a 5.56 case neck, not the bullet, so we needed to make ammo that mimicked the 5.56," Silvers said. "Existing bullets couldn't do it so we took the ground-up approach with the 115-grain OTM bullet, the lightest possible bullet weight without a polymer tip. It took nine extra months to design a bullet that was long enough to fill the magazine and hit the rib just right. The bullet ogive has to measure .256 inch in diameter at the rib to really work."

Other bullet companies like Barnes and Sierra (not a Freedom Group company) helped develop a complete suite of projectiles for multiple applications. Sierra's 125-grain MatchKing has the nose of a 210-grain MatchKing, a flat base and an overall length designed to work specifically in the .300 BLK. Engineers working on the Barnes 110-grain TAC-TX started at the point where the bullet touched the magazine rib and worked out both ends. For more on this bullet see page 104.

Why a flat base on open-tip match bullets and not the more common boat tail?

"In our testing, flat-base bullets have proven more accurate because gases are less likely to disrupt the bullet," Silvers said. "The effect seems more pronounced in short, nine-inch barrels. A boat tail would also protrude into the case, limiting capacity."

Silvers always thought the cost of loaded ammo is one of the factors that limited the Whisper's popularity. Working with Remington and Barnes, the Blackout was introduced with both higher-end hunting and match options and an affordable load that runs eleven dollars.

"It's cheaper than .30-30," Silvers said. "It's not as cheap as 5.56, but it uses a much bigger bullet."

All of Remington's brass is double struck to NATO hardness standards and on some cases the annealing marks are not polished out, providing the military (and civilian shooter) with visual proof the cartridge was annealed.

CARTRIDGE CONFUSION

With the obvious similarities between the .300 Blackout and .300 Whisper, there has been a tremendous amount of confusion as to interchangeability and, well, everything else. For an excellent story on the exact differences between the two, I would encourage you to read Steve Johnson's "Shades of Gray," a comprehensive cartridge comparison that ran in the November 2012 issue of "American Rifleman." (You can read this article at americanrifleman.org/articles/shades-of-gray/.)

While the cartridges obviously are very similar, there are important differences. Remington doesn't make ammo unless it is SAAMI approved, since it sets the standard for firearms and other ammo manufacturers to follow, eliminating safety concerns. There are quite a few wildcats with the Fireball name, so .30/221 Fireball wouldn't have worked since anything with that name would have to work in the new chamber. Remington probably could not have licensed the .300 Whisper name from SSK Industries and SAAMI wouldn't have allowed a trademarked name anyway. Further, there are a handful of different chamber reamers floating around with the Whisper name—SSK's version and a European CIP version, which had a tighter throat, just to name two—all with different dimensions. It was easier to start from scratch.

"To use the name would have limited our design," Silvers said. "People have also said we just took the drawing and changed it enough to avoid the patent. There is no patent on the Whisper, rather a trademark.

Besides, "whisper" is what you do in the library. We wanted a name that sounded tactical. Fireball implies a bright flash of light and that obviously wouldn't have worked. Eventually we settled on Blackout, since we had the name for the flash suppressor already."

The Blackout's throat is designed to work around the longest bullet used, a Sierra 220-grain MatchKing, giving it a .010-inch jump to the lands. The Blackout's neck diameter is slightly larger than the Whisper, allowing shooters to use fire-formed 5.56 cases.

"We kept same head space position as .221 Fireball, but the datum position fell on a radius and we changed that to fall on a straight area," Silvers said. "From there backward, it's exactly the same as a .221 Fireball."

So from the inventor of the cartridge, here is the scoop on interchangeability: "You can generally shoot Whisper cartridges in a Blackout chamber, but not the other way around because of the throat length," Silvers said. "It is very much like .223 and 5.56 in that regard. The shorter throat of some Whisper chambers could cause pressure issues with Blackout ammunition."

Hornady, the largest producer of Blackout ammo behind Remington, loads their ammo with the Whisper head stamp within the specifications for the Blackout cartridge. According to SAAMI, there are only two ways to properly mark a rifle: 300 AAC Blackout or .300 BLK. The metric designation is 7.62x35mm.

Several Freedom Group companies including Barnes worked on everything from rifles to bullets. The excellent 110-grain TAC-TX was just one of those developments.

RIFLES

For the most part, the military provided the development team with some basic parameters and left the make of rifles up to them, so long as they worked. Silvers said the rifles really came before the ammo and there was a lot of experimentation with gas system length and port size. The idea of a custom magazine was quickly scrapped, hence the tremendous amount of previously mentioned bullet development. It was also decided early on to use a standard spring and H2 buffer.

"We used high-speed video and studied bolt-carrier velocity to optimize the gas flow to achieve a certain bolt-carrier velocity," Silvers said. "The bolt velocity and cyclic rate stay within what Colt specifies for the M4 and all four configurations shoot between 700 and 950 rpm."

Sixteen-inch guns get a mid-length gas system to delay unlocking for an extra millisecond or two to reduce extractor force, just like in their 5.56 counterparts. This proved unreliable in rifles with barrels shorter than 16 inches, so SBRs use a pistol-length system. And pistol-length systems run both subsonic and supersonic ammo

Robert Silvers' original concept rifle used in the development of the .300 AAC Blackout.

because the subsonic loads generate enough gas. Both 16- and SBR-length rifles and uppers built by AAC are capable of reliable function in all four modes: supersonic/suppressed, supersonic/unsuppressed, subsonic/suppressed, subsonic/unsuppressed.

The correct gas port size depends on which buffer is used. With an H2 buffer, the nine-inch SBRs require a larger port for more gas. The exact size is proprietary information. Silvers said some early barrels were released from other companies with the wrong port size, leading to reliability issues.

Rifles, correctly built, have proven extremely reliable in my personal experience. I would associate any failures to feed more with bullet type, specifically polymer tips in heavier weights, than any intrinsic reliability issues with a rifle and magazine. Silvers has conducted extensive testing obviously and found the rifles meet reliability standards during semi- and full automatic fire.

DOES IT HAVE A FUTURE?

Silvers did confirm that both rifles and ammunition have been delivered to the "military customer" for testing and that additional units have requested and received prototypes for their own testing. And Silvers went on to describe the military's feedback as "extraordinary."

"Other military groups have started testing it, with completely different roles in mind," Silvers said. "It has expanded from the original concept."

Some have opined that the .300 BLK would be an ideal replacement for the 5.56 NATO. While the Blackout is a more efficient cartridge (19 grains of propellant compared to 26 grains in a 5.56), more easily suppressed and provides greater lethality even with barrels as short as nine inches, Silvers was still realistic about the 5.56's sticking power.

"It's not going to replace the 5.56," Silvers said. "But anyone who has special requirements for suppressed

DoD Photo

use or wants AK-like performance will want this cartridge. I could see it replacing four or five existing weapon systems. I could see it replacing the Heckler & Koch MP5SD because it is as quiet with three times the range and accuracy. It could also replace the MP7, since the point of that was to penetrate armor. It could replace the Mk18, too. It's not very efficient and Blackout is."

What is absolutely certain is how the cartridge and rifles have taken the AR-15 world by storm. Over the years a bunch of other-than-5.56 cartridges have been introduced and splashed or sputtered. Some like the 6.5mm Grendel quietly plod along adding a new shooter or two each day. Currently 160 companies make products associated with the .300 BLK, including dozens of rifle and ammunition manufacturers. And that's just a year after its introduction. Trijicon has produced a .300 caliber-specific ACOG, EOTech a holographic sight, and Leupold a scope. If the military never bought a single rifle or round, one would still have to consider the Blackout an unqualified success.

Rifle and ammo manufacturers immediately saw an opportunity to market the .300 BLK to hunters and camo rifles and hunting ammo saw concurrent introductions with tactical equipment. I have used the .300 BLK to kill both whitetail deer and feral hogs and would choose it, when paired with the 110-grain Barnes load, over most any .223 or 5.56 load.

Bristling at the notion that the Blackout is a niche cartridge, Silvers said the round is extremely versatile.

"It's the opposite of a niche cartridge because it has so many different potential applications," Silvers said. "If the .223 is the 9mm, the .300 BLK is .40 S&W. And ammo is plentiful and inexpensive."

It took two long years of development work to sort out complicated problems and adapt it for existing systems. Prototypes are now in the hands of "military customers," many having deployed. Commercially, Blackout rifles and ammunition are appearing and disappearing from dealer shelves. The .300 AAC BLK has arrived, and it looks like this .30-caliber dynamo is here to stay.

BY **PATRICK SWEENEY**
PHOTOS BY **MIKE ANSCHUETZ**
&
SSK INDUSTRIES

*None of this was easy,
or straightforward.*

THE

Whisper 300

STORY

I remember the day well.

Cool, overcast, nearing sunset, and a friend of mine was having a bit of fun on the back range at Second Chance, in between runs on the Light Rifle Pop and Flop (LRPF). The LRPF comprised falling-steel plates, shaped like bowling pins, at 45, 55 and 90 yards. Ned had hauled a new-to-me AR out of his truck (the group of us who had been contesting for loot and glory for years could recognize each other's rifles) and started on the far pin rack. At the first *Thup... Whack* I figured he was using a rimfire of some kind. Then I caught sight of the empty tumbling out of its ejection port. It was far too large to be a rimfire.

So I ambled over and picked up a case. *Wow, that's a short case with a big mouth on it*, I thought. I also noticed that the sound of the shot was softer than the sound of the impacts, either on the pins or on the timber glacis in front of the rack.

When he paused, I asked what this new thing was. "Oh, it's something J.D. is working on." In a curious bit of illogical logic, that explained everything while explaining nothing. We all had at least a nodding acquaintance with J.D. He was the mad scientist of the firearms industry and came up with cartridge ideas faster than we could even grasp them. His cartridges were different, performed like mad, and everyone knew that anything he worked on had all the details thrashed, tested, determined and settled. "So, what does it do?" With a conspiratorial look, he remarked, "It throws Sierra 240s subsonic, and you don't have to do anything to an AR but change barrels."

J.D. Jones with one of the first sub-gun versions of the .300 Whisper. First military sales were in the mid-'90s, and all were 10-inch suppressed with a two-point can.

This rifle is the most popular suppressed version with civilians: 16½-inch barrel, SSK two-point attachment suppressor that fits within the forend.

That was early enough in the R&D process—1991 or 1992—that the world had not yet heard of the .300 Whisper, but I determined that I would get myself one of them as soon as possible. Unfortunately, as soon as possible ended up being 2011.

The origins of the .300 Whisper are not entirely clear, but for being the latest tactical "must have," one thing is certain: It came to us from the firing line of metallic silhouette ranges. And pretty early on, too. In order to get to the bottom of this story, I took a scenic drive through eastern Ohio to visit J.D. Despite not having talked to him for some few years, he was happy to see me and happy to see what he could recall.

The origins are obvious in some regards: "I took the cartridge from metallic silhouette shooters, and when I was working out the dimensions and other details, we tested it on steel. It has enough residual energy to take rams off the stands, no problem." The task he set himself was not at all easy. You see, the original, prehistoric Whisper was known as the .300-221, that is, simply a .221 Fireball cartridge necked up to .30 caliber. When it was a wildcat, everyone who wanted one could have a chambering reamer of any dimension they wanted. Since the resulting .300-221 was going to be used in a Thompson/Center Contender, and each competitor used his brass and no one else's, dimensional stability between reamers and dies was not at all something they concerned themselves with. Let's be clear about this: While you may own or buy a barrel or rifle that is marked ".300-221," there is no guarantee that its dimensions are anything close to what we now call the .300 Whisper.

What J.D. had to do was refine the cartridge and determine what dimensions mattered when it was to be in the AR-15 platform and what dimensions didn't. What problems, you ask? Let's start with brass.

J.D. was almost proud of the horror stories that came with this project. "One of the first things we learned was that you couldn't open up the necks of .221 Fireball brass in any kind of volume and stay profitable or sane. Such a high percentage of them had tilted necks, bulged shoulders, split necks and so on that the loss rate was too high. And if you went slower, you couldn't make enough to keep up, even then." Remember those metallic silhouette shooters? If you're using a .300-221 to topple steel, you don't need more than a hundred cases. If it takes you a weekend of work to craft them, so what? J.D. wasn't thinking like a competitive handloader, he was concerned about volume.

I asked, "So, why not just cut off .223 brass and neck that down?" With a grin, J.D. told me, "That was even worse. While the neck dimensions of .223 or 5.56 brass are closely controlled, the internal taper isn't. So you cut off the brass and find the resulting neck is too thick or so out-of-round it can't chamber once you seat a round. At the peak of testing, I had a chart showing over 200 .223 and 5.56 headstamps that would work and nearly 40 that wouldn't."

And that's how it came to pass that SSK Industries had to bite the bullet and order up .300 brass, made specifically for the Whisper. When it comes to research and testing, J.D. is not one to leave a stone unturned. He tells me he had put 20,000 rounds of R&D ammo through various firearms before he said a word to anyone about it. He ordered components and ammo in volume. And soon after it became known, it was listed in "Jane's Ammunition Handbook" and the whole world (at least, those who could afford "Jane's") knew about it.

Dennis Lawrence, SSK Gunsmith, put the first AR upper together.

A very early experimental night sight-TV recording and broadcasting camera mounted on an early SSK M16 that was suppressed in .300 Whisper. You could watch the bullet's flight.

When SSK does custom, they don't do anything but hand-fitted precision. This rifle receiver is having its new barrel threads cut to fit exactly—not chased to a production fit.

When it comes to nearly silent cartridges, J.D. came up with more than just the .300 Whisper. In bullet diameters, he has Whisper-named cartridges from 6mm up to .510, and the parent cases are as small as the .30 Luger and as large as the .338 Lapua and .460 Weatherby. Well, the Lapua and Weatherby cases are the starting point, but by the time J.D. is done with them, they've been shortened, re-formed, blown out and otherwise made to perform as he expects them to.

You may ask, ".30 Luger? .50 caliber?" When J.D. gets an idea, he applies it across the entire spectrum. Yes, a 9mm can be suppressed, but doing it in a Luger case offers options that a 9mm does not. And the .50? Actually, the several flavors of .50? The performance is eye-opening. While the ratio of muzzle blast to bullet impact in a .300 Whisper is noticeable, the ratio from a .50 or .510 Whisper is almost alarming.

Once he'd worked out the details of the .300 Whisper, J.D. then did as he had typically done: gotten the reloading die manufacturers to make dies for him, chambered T/C barrels in the cartridge and offered them for sale through his company, SSK Industries. However, the .300 Whisper proved to be something else, something with much more legs. Specialized cartridges, in single-shot handguns like the T/C, have a certain demographic.

As he had done with all of his other cartridges, J.D. trademarked the .300 Whisper cartridge and name. A trademarked name was not a problem when dealing with the single-shot cohorts, but the volume that ARs brought to the table was overwhelming. SSK had their hands full simply in getting orders for brass and loaded ammo to their supplier, then shipping it on to eager customers.

The bottleneck was simple. The American standards organization, SAAMI, had a long-standing policy against accepting a trademarked cartridge. Without SAAMI acceptance, the heavy hitters in the industry would not manufacture a cartridge with their name as part of their catalog offering. They could not. If J.D. was to market the Whisper, he had to contract with a manufacturer to make it as his and pay the full freight of setup, manufacture and shipping.

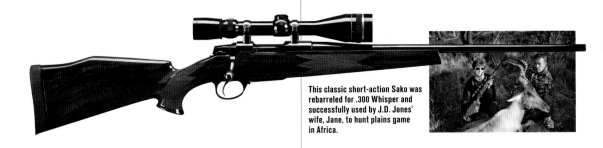

This classic short-action Sako was rebarreled for .300 Whisper and successfully used by J.D. Jones' wife, Jane, to hunt plains game in Africa.

The demographic of the AR back in the mid- to late-1990s was a certain set of tactically minded shooters. Suppressors were not as common. You could travel the country and not see suppressors in use. The Federal Assault Weapon Ban of 1994 put ARs on everyone's wish list. By the time the sun had set on the AWB/94, everyone who wanted one—it seems—had a suppressor. And by 2004 everyone wanted to own an AR-15. There was no longer a hope of keeping up with demand, this despite the .300 Whisper having been a standing order with his supplier.

I have to admit, my first encounter with the .300 Whisper set me on a slightly incorrect path. I had been working under the assumption for the longest time that the .300 was meant from the start to be a suppressed cartridge and that the supersonic loadings were simply a wildcat-of-a-wildcat, as it were. Not so. J.D. had recognized from the start that it was a super-efficient cartridge and had worked on supersonic loadings alongside the subsonics. While looking over his rifle racks, he showed me a rifle he'd built on a short-action Sako, chambered in .300 Whisper, that his wife had used to slay all that walked before her on a trip to Africa. OK, she didn't shoot a Cape buff, but who would do that with any .30 rifle? But all manner of antelope fell and fell hard.

No visit could be complete without looking over R&D samples, testing rifles and trying this or that suppressor on the end. Fast, slow, light, heavy, select fire, semi-auto—it was a Whisper-fest. Plus, one trick J.D. worked out when designing his .300 Whisper barrel is the switchable gas port. You can change your gas system from supersonic hunting ammo to subsonic heavyweights and have them both work. While I've had a lot of .300 Whisper experience lately, some of the other calibers were new to me. After hammering out a magazine of suppressed, subsonic .458 SOCOM to cap the range session, I was

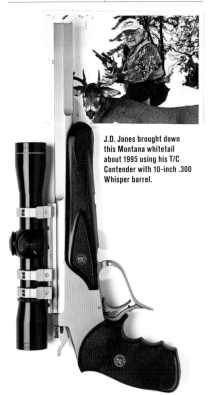

J.D. Jones brought down this Montana whitetail about 1995 using his T/C Contender with 10-inch .300 Whisper barrel.

ready for a break. Sometimes too much of a good thing is too much in select fire.

I asked J.D. what he might tell his younger self, if he'd a chance. He wanted to think about it, so a few days later he sent me his reply in an e-mail.

"Frankly, that is a pretty tough question. After thinking about it for a day off and on, there isn't really a great deal I would do to effect change in my life. Certainly, I was very näive going into the firearms business. I did not realize there were so many unethical and dishonest people in the industry, as well as some of the finest people who ever walked on the face of the earth. I would certainly advise taking all steps possible to protect anything invented that I did not do partially due to bad advice from some in the industry and also attorneys.

"When SSK started to really take off, Jane and I discussed the future of the business and decided to keep it small, high quality with a few highly skilled and dedicated employees and do our best to enjoy life. I would never change that. SSK is not a job. It is doing something I love every day and making a lot of people happy with the products and seeing their achievements using it is quite satisfying. It has given me the ability and opportunity to be involved in a lot of interesting things in a lot of interesting places. All in all, it has been a helluva good run. Why change anything?"

So there you have it; if you rate cartridge efficiency by how much powder it takes to generate useful velocity, it would be hard to beat the .300 Whisper. That it uses perhaps the most common, easiest-to-locate bullet diameter in America—the .308—is a bonus. If a gun shop prides itself on having any reloading components at all, they'll certainly have something in .308.

If the hot fever of cartridge design ever hits you, resign yourself to one fact: J.D. Jones has probably already been there.

PART III
AMMO & COMPONENTS

ACTIVE AND RECENTLY SEPERATED MILITARY AND LAW ENFORCEMENT PROFESSIONALS RESPOND TO OUR SURVEY AND DESCRIBE THEIR PREFERRED ONE-GUN OUTFIT.

SU

VEY SAYS

COMPILED BY GLORIA SHYTLES

BOOK OF THE AR-15 wanted to know how experienced professionals carry America's favorite black rifle. We started by identifying and questioning our own professional connections. As the responses grew more intriguing, we then sought to expand this survey to include hundreds of other respected warfighters and public defenders. Each of these respondents earns his living while serving with an AR-type rifle, either active military, law enforcement, firearms instructors, armorers, government contractors, combat veterans or in similar fields of interest. Some statements may seem like no-brainers, while others took us by surprise. Review and decide for yourself.

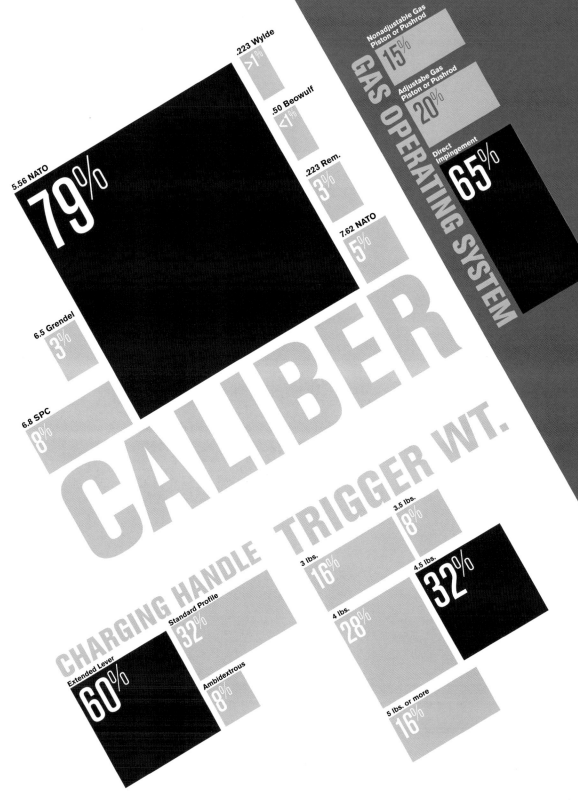

CALIBER

.223 Wylde
>1%

.50 Beowulf
<1%

5.56 NATO
79%

.223 Rem.
3%

7.62 NATO
5%

6.5 Grendel
3%

6.8 SPC
8%

GAS OPERATING SYSTEM

Nonadjustable Gas Piston or Pushrod
15%

Adjustabe Gas Piston or Pushrod
20%

Direct Impingement
65%

CHARGING HANDLE

Standard Profile
32%

Extended Lever
60%

Ambidextrous
8%

TRIGGER WT.

3.5 lbs.
8%

3 lbs.
16%

4 lbs.
28%

4.5 lbs.
32%

5 lbs. or more
16%

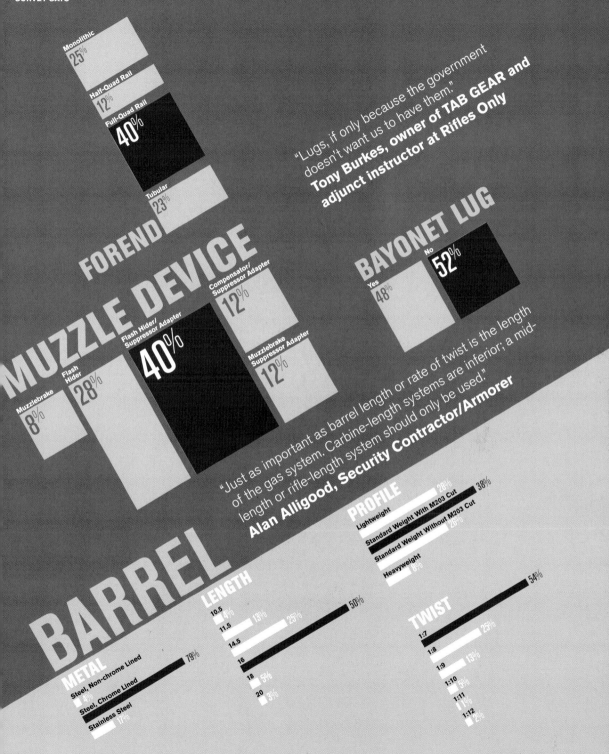

FOREND

Monolithic
25%

Half-Quad Rail
12%

Full-Quad Rail
40%

Tubular
23%

"Lugs, if only because the government doesn't want us to have them."
Tony Burkes, owner of TAB GEAR and adjunct instructor at Rifles Only

BAYONET LUG

Yes
48%

No
52%

MUZZLE DEVICE

Muzzlebrake
8%

Flash Hider
28%

Flash Hider/Suppressor Adapter
40%

Compensator/Suppressor Adapter
12%

Muzzlebrake Suppressor Adapter
12%

"Just as important as barrel length or rate of twist is the length of the gas system. Carbine-length systems are inferior; a mid-length or rifle-length system should only be used!"
Alan Alligood, Security Contractor/Armorer

BARREL

PROFILE

Lightweight
28%

Standard Weight With M203 Cut
38%

Standard Weight Without M203 Cut
26%

Heavyweight
8%

LENGTH

10.5
4%

11.5
13%

14.5
25%

16
50%

18
5%

20
3%

TWIST

1:7
54%

1:8
25%

1:9
13%

1:10
3%

1:11
1%

1:12
2%

METAL

Steel, Non-chrome Lined
4%

Steel, Chrome Lined
79%

Stainless Steel
17%

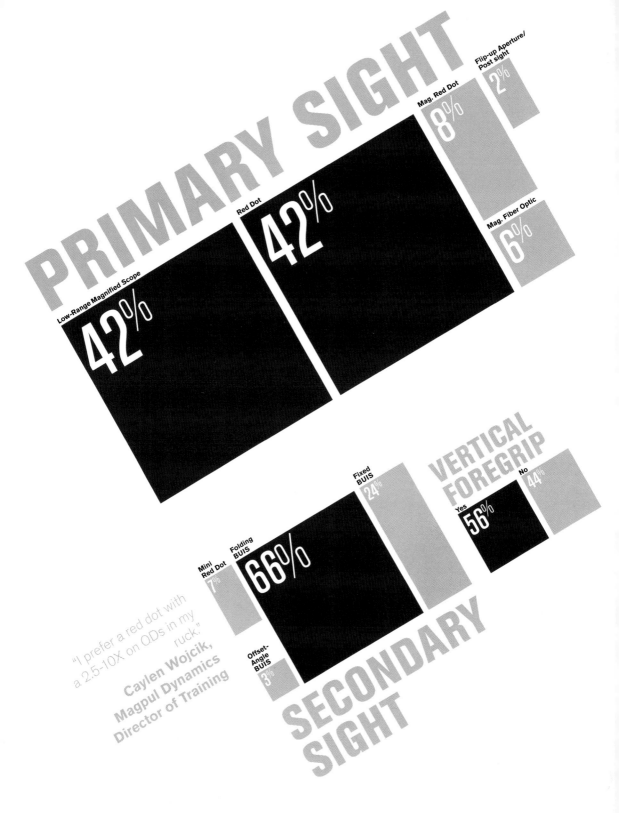

PRIMARY SIGHT

Low-Range Magnified Scope
42%

Red Dot
42%

Mag. Red Dot
8%

Flip-up Aperture/Post sight
2%

Mag. Fiber Optic
6%

SECONDARY SIGHT

Mini Red Dot
7%

Folding BUIS
66%

Fixed BUIS
24%

Offset-Angle BUIS
3%

VERTICAL FOREGRIP

Yes
56%

No
44%

"I prefer a red dot with a 2.5-10X on QDs in my ruck."

Caylen Wojcik,
Magpul Dynamics
Director of Training

WEAPON LIGHT

Yes **100**%

COLOR

Black **68**%

Flat Dark Earth/Tan **18**%

Other **5**%

OD Green **9**%

STOCK

Collapsible **100**%

"30. It's a lot of rounds, but not so much that your magazines are too bulky or heavy that they become a distraction."

Anonymous, U.S. Army Special Forces

MAGAZINE CAPACITY

Round **32**%

30 Round **65**%

60 Round **3**%

LASER DESIGNATOR

Yes **54**%

No **46**%

SLING

One Point **17**%

Two Point **79**%

Three Point **4**%

RAIL COVERS

None **40**%

Rubber Filler **52**%

Panels **8**%

TRIGGER

Great ergonomics, match-winning accuracy and unfaltering reliability are but a few of the AR platform's finer points. One area in which the AR has room for improvement is its trigger. The original two-stage AR trigger's bad reputation is deserved. The original design was built to withstand being dropped from helicopters and abused by grunts. The design features that allow it to pass stringent military safety guidelines make it impossible to achieve a light, safe trigger pull.

In the early days, gunsmiths did their best to tune AR triggers. To do so, they had to reduce the amount of sear engagement, which required some careful stoning. Unfortunately, the 8620 steel those early triggers were made of was simply case-hardened. Case-hardening is just a surface treatment, so those ambitious tinkerers quickly filed their way down to the ductile portion of the steel. It didn't take long for those tuned sears to wear, and the affected rifles would double. As fun as it is to send two rounds downrange with every pull of the trigger, it isn't safe, and the ATF frowns on the practice.

Today's AR shooters are quite fortunate. The tremendous rise in 3-Gun competition and the incredible popularity of the AR platform have driven some really talented folks to bring out some fantastic

HAPPY

BY **GREG RODRIGUEZ**
PHOTOS BY **LANCE BERTOLINO**

How to acheive the best results from every trigger squeeze.

AR triggers. I've been fortunate enough to try several of these triggers over the last few years. I also count top gunsmiths such as George Gardner and KK Jense among my friends. Between us, we've installed and shot most of the AR-15 triggers on the market. Here is our take on the AR triggers with which we have enough collective experience to give a meaningful rating.

GEISSELE AUTOMATICS

Geissele Automatics makes 11 rugged triggers for a variety of applications. Its SSA (Super Semi-Automatic) trigger is the semiauto version of the select-fire trigger Geissele makes for U.S. SOCOM. The nonadjustable trigger was designed for hard use in a battlefield environment. I own several of them, and they are, indeed, excellent triggers. The trigger I chose to review is the S3G (Super 3-Gun) trigger.

Like all Geissele's triggers, the S3G is made of S7 tool steel. S7 is a shock-resistant steel used to make battering tools, punches and chisels—exactly the kind of repetitive battering to which AR hammers and sears are subjected. To increase wear resistance, Geissele vacuum heat treats, double tempers and cryogenically treats each part. A full-power hammer spring ensures reliability, and the sear is wire-EDM cut for an even smoother trigger pull. The result is a practically bombproof AR trigger with an incredible feel and light pull.

The S3G's pull is, in Geissele parlance, a hybrid. That is to say

A good aftermarket trigger can make an AR that initially appears to be an MOA rifle perform like a sub-MOA rifle. Perceived accuracy isn't based solely on the manufactured qualities of a rifle's components, but the shooter's ability to best apply the fundamentals of marksmanship—including a skillful trigger pull.

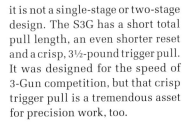

it is not a single-stage or two-stage design. The S3G has a short total pull length, an even shorter reset and a crisp, 3½-pound trigger pull. It was designed for the speed of 3-Gun competition, but that crisp trigger pull is a tremendous asset for precision work, too.

My first experience with Geissele triggers was an SSA model I installed a year or so ago in one of my ARs, a super-accurate carbine from American Spirit Arms. The gun shot under a half inch with several loads, but I had trouble doing it consistently because of its heavy trigger pull. The Geissele fixed that problem,

but the installation was a bit tougher than many hobbyists should tackle.

Because I struggled with it a bit the first time, when it was time to install an S3G trigger in my custom DPMS, I sent it to George Gardner. George is quite fond of Geissele triggers, giving them high marks for consistent pulls and durability. However,

Photos by Lance Bertolino

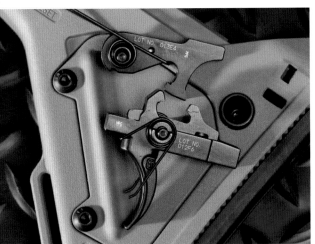

Geissele's triggers are noted for their durability. In fact, they are the trigger of choice for U.S. SOCOM. If those guys can't break them, neither can you.

JP Enterprises' original trigger has perhaps the cleanest pull of the bunch. However, it is a bit difficult to install and adjust.

he agreed that installation can be problematic for the inexperienced. KK Jense said the pull was not as good as some other triggers. He ranked it third for trigger pull and ease of installation, but first in reliability and durability. I didn't have to install it, but I love its clean, consistent pull and durable construction. I also place a great deal of trust in my Geissele triggers. If they can stand up to the abuse our Special Forces operators heap on them, I know they're tough enough for me.

JP ENTERPRISES

Like other quality units, the JP trigger is made of hardened A2 tool steel. The trigger itself is cast from A2 steel, while the hammer and sear are machined from bar stock. Critical engagement features on the hammer and sear are EDM-burned for the smoothest possible trigger pull, while the rest of the cuts are done with a laser.

The JP trigger also features some major design improvements on the original AR trigger. Most notably,

TRIGGER COMPARISON

Trigger	Pull (lbs)	Ease of Installation*	Reliability*	Design	MSRP
Geissele S3G	3 lb., 5 oz.	8	10	Hybrid	$230
JP	3 lb., 9 oz.	7	9	Single-stage	$120
Rock River	4 lb., 10 oz.	9	9	Two-stage	$120
Timney	3 lb., 2 oz.	10	8	Single-stage	$195
Wilson	2 lb., 15 oz.	10	10	Single-stage	$270

*Rankings of Ease of Installation and Reliability are the opinioned rating observed, averaged and assigned to those triggers by the author, George Gardner and KK Jense on a scale of one to 10, with 10 being the best possible score.

the sear geometry was changed so the hammer reset takes just two degrees of travel, rather than eight degrees. It travels less, so it generates less speed. Consequently, there is less wear on the hammer, and the hammer cannot gain enough velocity to damage the sear. The JP also has engagement and overtravel adjustments, and the design eliminates disconnector timing issues that can lead to doubling. The result of all those design changes is a great trigger pull that lasts.

The JP trigger kit comes with an installation CD and several different spring combinations to give you a trigger pull that ranges

from three pounds on up to 4½ pounds. The one I use most has a red hammer spring and yellow trigger spring. This combination yields a trigger pull in the 3½- to four-pound range but sacrifices nothing in terms of reliability or durability. The heavier hammer spring also allows it to work just fine with .308 ARs.

I have several such JP triggers on various ARs. All features crisp, clean trigger pulls with almost nonexistent takeup, minimal overtravel and a very short reset. Those qualities work well for speed and precision work. However, as much as I like it, the JP trigger is probably not a trigger a

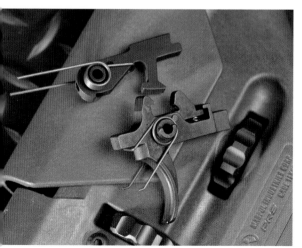

Rock River's NM two-stage tactical trigger is robust, affordable and easy to install. It is a substantial upgrade for any carbine.

The modular Timney trigger got high marks for its ease of installation and excellent trigger pull.

beginner should install. KK and George agreed; both gave the JP the lowest score for ease of installation but gave its consistent, creep-free trigger pull the highest marks.

ROCK RIVER NM TWO-STAGE TACTICAL

Rock River's two-stage trigger is an OCMP-legal, match-grade trigger. It is known for an excellent pull and great quality, despite an MSRP of just $120. The trigger isn't a modular design, but it is an easy install if you have any experience working on ARs. After disassembly, simply replace your factory hammer and trigger assembly with the Rock River parts. The trigger is pre-adjusted at the factory, so there is no fitting or adjusting necessary.

I have the Rock River trigger on several of my ARs, including a custom AR-10 built by George Gardner. When I asked George why he used it, he said the Rock River unit is one of his favorite go switches. He occasionally has to work out a burr or rough edge, but they are usually good to go right out of the package, don't cost an arm and a leg, and are easy to install. When you build as many ARs as George, it's great testimony that he is so fond of them.

TIMNEY

Timney's triggers are instantly recognizable thanks to their gold trigger housing and modular, drop-in design. They are wildly popular due to their great trigger pull, reasonable MSRP of $195 and incredibly easy installation.

Timney's triggers are set at the factory at three, four or 4½ pounds. To install one, simply remove your gun's trigger assembly, drop in the Timney, reinsert your old trigger pins and tighten a couple

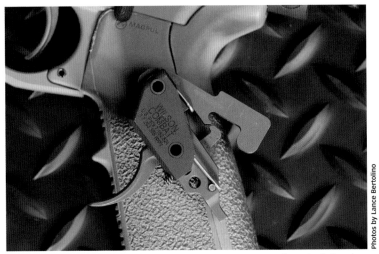

Wilson Combat's TTU is available in single- or two-stage versions. Both have a pull of four pounds and are among the easiest AR triggers to install thanks to their modular design. They are also extremely durable.

of hex screws at the bottom of the assembly. There is no need to tune or adjust the trigger, and the proprietary design eliminates pin rotation.

Timney's AR-15 trigger is not just a pretty trigger with a light pull. The trigger housing is machined from rugged 6061 T6 aluminum, and the hammer is machined from high-quality tool steel. All the steel parts are hardened to 56-60 Rockwell to prevent them from wearing prematurely or breaking, so parts wear and doubling are not issues.

I've installed Timney triggers in two of my ARs. All have a tiny bit of takeup, and none breaks at its advertised weight, but they are all within a few ounces and every one of them has worked with 100 percent reliability in my guns. I have seen a friend's new Timney double, but the company made it right. It's not a common problem, but it has happened.

Gunsmiths George Gardner of GA Precision and KK Jense of Jense Precision agreed that the Timney is one of the easiest triggers to

install. However, George stated that the triggers are not as consistent as some other models, and KK ranked them below the other triggers in this review for the feel of the trigger pull. They scored well, but were not as highly regarded in terms of durability and feel as the other triggers in the test.

WILSON COMBAT

Wilson's Tactical Trigger Unit (TTU) is an incredibly easy-to-install, modular, single- or two-stage trigger. The completely self-contained design has no parts or screws to lose or adjust. Simply remove your factory trigger and hammer and drop in the modular Wilson part for a crisp, four-pound trigger pull.

The TTU's hammer, trigger and sear are either precision CNC-machined or Wire EDM-cut from solid H13 bar stock that is heat treated for durability. The hammer, trigger and disconnector pivot on hardened-steel bushings to eliminate wear and stress on the receiver pin holes and pins. Unique hammer geometry guarantees reliable ignition,

This custom DPMS AR has a Geissele trigger. It has served the author well for several thousand rounds and has an excellent pull.

and a 1911-style half-cock notch enables the TTU to meet or exceed military drop safety requirements without sacrificing feel.

KK Jense installed a single-stage TTU on a custom carbon-barreled carbine he built for me recently. I was impressed with the quality of the pull, which broke at the advertised four pounds with nary a hint of creep and an incredibly short reset. The trigger feels great and is easy to shoot accurately at speed. KK rated it very high in feel, reliability and ease of installation. After removing and reinstalling the unit myself and putting about 1,800 rounds downrange with it, I would have to agree.

CHOOSING A TRIGGER

If you're looking for an easy way to wring a bit more accuracy out of your favorite AR or pick up a bit of speed from your competition gun, a replacement trigger is a quick and easy fix. It may not cure all your speed and accuracy woes, but you will be surprised at the difference a crisp, light, creep-free trigger pull can make in your scores. You'll have to consider your own needs and budget when selecting a trigger, but you can rest assured that any of the units covered here will provide years of trouble-free service.

GEISSELE | TRIGGERS

FROM THE GUY WHO FIGURED OUT HOW TO MAKE A MATCH-QUALITY TRIGGER COMBAT RELIABLE.

The best products in the firearms industry often come from avid shooters who get frustrated with their equipment and decide they can build something better.

In 2003, Bill Geissele was hot and heavy into shooting High Power rifle matches (where he earned his Distinguished Rifleman badge). Part of the course of fire for any High Power match is shooting offhand, the most difficult position to master. While sitting and kneeling certainly require skill, offhand (or standing) is the most unstable position from which to shoot and the most unforgiving.

Offhand shooting at the national level requires an exceptional trigger. If the trigger is too heavy, the shooter can easily pull the sights off the bullseye as the rifle fires. Triggers with creep make it difficult to know when they will break, so hitting the tiny bullseye becomes problematic. Last, triggers with excessive overtravel can induce movement in the milliseconds following the shot's break.

BY TOM BECKSTRAND

Back in 2003, there were two triggers that almost all of the serious competitors were using. Bill tried both and found that neither could meet his needs. The problems he encountered with the two-stage competitive triggers were that they would frequently lose their second stage and the pull would eventually become one gritty, homogenous 10-pound experience. Another frequent problem was that the "competition" springs would fatigue at unpredictable intervals. His rifle might meet match regulations one week and then be out of spec the next. Bill decided then that he was going to make himself "one good trigger" that he could use competitively.

NO CHERRIES HERE

Even in '03, Bill wasn't a novice when it came to making stuff. He'd been working in a machine shop since he was 15 years old and had studied engineering in college. He also had a successful career going at the time as the engineering manager of a design department

Bill Geissele shooting a High Power match circa 2002. Work on his trigger would begin the following year.

in the railway industry. Since he did design modeling at his day job already, he figured he had the skills to solve his trigger problem.

Turns out Bill was right. He bought a bundle of CAD modeling software and set up shop in the 12'x14' basement of his 1,800-square-foot house, where he still resides today. Other than wanting to solve the disappearing second stage and unpredictable spring weight problems, Bill wanted to address some other match-trigger deficiencies as well.

He wanted a trigger that could have its sear engagement surface and second-stage pull weight adjusted separately. Most adjustable triggers adjusted both simultaneously, so the shooter had to choose which one was more important than the other and could never get both exactly where they needed to be. He wanted to move the trigger bow $3/16$ of an inch forward to reduce crowding the trigger. Last, he wanted as fast a lock-time as he could get.

Fast lock-time is important on a trigger because the faster the lock-time, the closer the shot will impact to our last known aiming point. As the trigger breaks, we often lose the sights or reticle under recoil. For AR-type rifles, the massive Mil-Spec hammer has a slow lock-time because it's huge and flat and has much of its mass perpendicular to its travel arc. The mass is also positioned far from the axis about which it rotates.

Imagine that a Mil-Spec hammer striking the firing pin is like driving tent pegs with a cast-iron snow shovel. The large, flat mass of the hammer is slow to get moving and, once moving, wants to keep moving. The face of the hammer is very large and, when it impacts the firing pin, imparts substantial force into not only the firing pin but also everything the firing pin touches. We see this disturbance by dry firing our rifle and watching the front sight or reticle jump when the hammer slams home.

Bill Geissele's design is like driving tent pegs with a hammer; it's the right tool for the job. The hammer Geissele designed has a small face that contacts the firing pin and has its mass parallel to the hammer's travel arc and closer to its rotational axis. All of the hammer's mass is behind the face that contacts the firing pin. The advantages of his design are readily apparent when we compare the two hammers side by side.

With much less mass on his hammer, Bill found a way to guarantee delivery of more substantial force to the firing pin while cutting the lock-time in half. The Geissele 17-gram hammer on his match trigger has a lock-time of 4.4 milliseconds (the fastest for any AR trigger) versus the 10 milliseconds of the 29-gram hammer with the Mil-Spec model we all know. Bill's smaller hammer also wreaks considerably less chaos during that crucial moment when the trigger releases the sear and the hammer swings forward to contact the firing pin. Less mass equals less disturbance when it crashes home. Those 12 grams of fat Bill shaved from the Mil-Spec hammer represent a huge net increase in accuracy.

THE TWO-STAGE ADVANTAGE

AR triggers usually come in either single- or two-stage variations. Geissele triggers are almost all two-stage except for a hybrid model that has no discernable first stage with a really long and light second stage. The advantage of the two-stage trigger is that it offers safety, reliability, forgiveness and performance. When we go to single stage, we lose one or two of those four attributes.

Single-stage triggers release when we apply enough force to release the trigger from the sear and require no movement through a "prep" stage. This allows manufacturers to make really crisp triggers that barely have to move to fire, but it also mandates that the only contact between trigger and sear is probably around five to 10 thousands of an inch for a really good match single-stage trigger.

In order to get a nice, light trigger pull for our single-stage trigger, we also need light springs that don't keep a lot of tension on

This is what all the fuss is about. Triggers look simple enough, but the devil is in the details. Geissele triggers are precision EDM-cut from premium materials.

the trigger-sear engagement surface. The light spring is a joy to shoot, but it also means a slow lock-time. The lighter spring also means that the primer doesn't get smacked as hard as it normally would. Hard-core bench and High-Power shooters will tell you that primers need a consistent hard smack to ensure complete and rapid ignition of the cartridge's powder. Rapid and consistent powder ignition means less variation in muzzle velocity and less vertical stringing at distance. Smack that primer hard if you want maximum accuracy.

That small amount of trigger-sear contact in a single stage means that we better be ready to shoot when our finger touches the trigger. This requires some training discipline (which is a good thing) but also means that we need to be extra vigilant when we're tired or stressed. While we can all control our physical movement, it is difficult to always be sharp after we've been on the move for hours or days or during times when physical and psychological stress levels are high. In moments like these, two-stage triggers give us more control over when we fire our rifles.

A two-stage trigger has the trigger and sear slide across each other into their firing position during the first stage. This first stage lets us put our finger on the trigger and move it to where we want it without firing the rifle, much like we adjust the seat and mirrors when we get into a car before putting it in

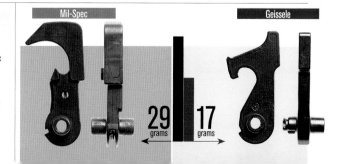

TRIGGER COMPARISON

The massive Mil-Spec hammer weighs 29 grams and has much of its mass far away from its rotational axis. These factors give it a pedestrian lock-time of 10 milliseconds. The Geissele hammer weighs 17 grams and has a lock-time of 4.4 milliseconds.

The large, flat face of the Mil-Spec hammer imparts considerable disturbance on the rifle when it impacts the firing pin. The Geissele hammer focuses all of its force directly into the firing pin.

Hi-Speed NM

HK-MR

Super Dynamic Combat

Super Semi-automatic Enhanced

Super Semi-automatic Trigger

Super 3 Gun

gear. The second stage then requires only an incremental increase in pressure to break the trigger-sear engagement and fire the rifle.

The advantage of the two-stage trigger is that the first stage has a fair amount of movement that is easy to feel and can have anywhere from two to four pounds of pull. This allows us to get set for a last, final, precise pull to fire the rifle. The second stage can have as little as six ounces of pull, so, in effect, we can safely get our felt pull weight down much lower with a two-stage trigger than a single stage.

THE FIRST TRIGGER
Bill started working on his trigger in 2003 and finished up in 2004. That first model he designed and used in 2004 was his Hi-Speed National Match trigger. It is the trigger that started the company, and it's still available today.

Once Bill completed his trigger and began competing with it, word spread quickly of the advantages it offered. He took his trigger to Camp Perry in 2004 and competed with it there. After he used it for the CMP matches, he got to talking with members of the Army Marksmanship Unit (AMU), who asked him details about the trigger. The armorer in charge of triggers asked Bill if it used a full-power hammer spring and told him that they only used full-power hammer springs because of the accuracy loss associated with under-powered springs. Bill said it did. The armorer asked to see his rifle and manipulated the trigger a few times before getting the attention of Lt. Col. Dave Liwanag, commander of the unit.

I got to know Dave while competing at the Army Small Arms Championships in 2006. He is a Special Forces officer, competitive shooter (Distinguished) and unadulterated lover of guns. Dave tried the trigger, looked at the armorer and said, "This is exactly what we need." Dave liked the trigger so much, Bill loaned it to him to use in the NRA matches at Perry that year.

Bill received a request from the AMU for six of his Hi-Speed National Match triggers in January 2005. He would later learn that those six triggers were used to build proof-of-concept rifles for the upcoming SASS/M110 solicitation. The AMU built the rifles for the Infantry Board at Fort Benning.

Once the AMU-built rifles validated the concept, history tells us that Knight's Arma-

ment won the solicitation and that they used their own trigger for the M110. The Sniper Training Detachment of 3rd Special Forces Group did part of the testing of the M110 at Fort Bragg. My former teammate was the NCOIC of the detachment and later told me that the triggers of the M110 were a "Knightmare," with many losing screws up on the gun line. If only they'd kept the Geissele … . This wasn't the end of trigger problems for our Special Operations guys.

Bill's next contact from the Army came in 2006 when members of a select unit within the Special Operation community asked him if they could take a look at his trigger. It seems that one of their two-stage match triggers failed in combat while the men were riding in an armored vehicle. Accidental discharges are taken very seriously within this unit, and if the operator is found guilty of negligence, that man is dismissed from the unit, even if he's been there for years. It is the sin for which there is no forgiveness.

The results of the very thorough investigation concluded that the disconnector failed, allowing the rifle to fire. The unit concluded that this was a design flaw with the trigger in question and began to look for a replacement. The trigger they wanted to replace the flawed two stage would be a select-fire model that could still be used for precision. Bill put his talents to work, and in December 2006 he handed over his Super-Select Fire (SSF) for field testing.

THE COMPANY GROWS
With field testing of the SSF underway, Bill got invited to the customer's facility to speak with their gunsmiths and armorers. The purpose of the meeting was to educate Bill on the customer's needs based on what they'd seen with their triggers over the course of millions of rounds and several years of intense combat. Bill listened and learned about all the problems associated with getting a trigger to work in combat, where it's subjected to hard use, corrosion and debris. He took good notes and went home to build more triggers.

Bill's SSF was adopted for use in the summer of 2007. The original triggers he submitted for field testing are still being used; one trigger now has more than 150,000 rounds on it. That particular trigger and

Super Dynamic
3 Gun

lower receiver is on its third upper and still going strong.

As part of his expansion, Bill decided to remove the auto-sear features of the SSF and the SSA was born. Crane (the guys who build many of the weapons in the Special Operations community) has since safety certified the SSA for use in both the Mk11 and Mk12.

Other models arrived in quick succession. The SSA-E has slightly different sear geometry than the SSA, so the pull is lighter and the break is very crisp. It is a trigger designed for precision use in combat. The S3G came next. Bill took his SSA and modified it for a customer that wanted a "single stage." Bill changed the sear geometry to eliminate the first stage and cut the weight of the second stage in half. It's like a Glock trigger on ball bearings. The Super Dynamic line came into existence because the straight trigger bow gives the impression of a lighter pull. Last, the Super TRICON is a trigger designed with the input of former Navy SEAL Jeff Gonzales. The trigger bow has a shallower curve and is grooved to accommodate shooting with gloves.

Super Dynamic
Enhanced

TRIGGER TIME

Preparing to write this article, I spent some time getting to know Geissele triggers. I put the Hi-Speed National Match in my LaRue OBR and think it's the greatest trigger I've ever used in an AR-pattern rifle. The first stage is right around three pounds, and I have the second stage set at just under one pound. It is perfect for precision use without being fragile or overly sensitive to incidental contact.

I've also tried the SSA, SSA-E and S3G triggers. All have their place, and I encourage AR shooters to get to know the product line. I would also like to point out that Bill has done some terrific work with AR forends, an endeavor that began when the same Special Operations client asked him if he could build a forend for their HK 416s. The forends are extremely well made, and the number of rails Bill makes continues to grow.

It's hard to imagine that an entire company came into existence because Bill Geissele got sick of failing triggers in competition. With the talents he cultivated over his life and an incredible work ethic, he's managed to become the premier manufacturer of AR-pattern triggers and has recently turned his attention to forends. Bill's meteoric rise didn't happen by accident. Once you get your hands on some of his products, you'll understand how it all happened so fast.

Super-Select
Fire

Super TRICON

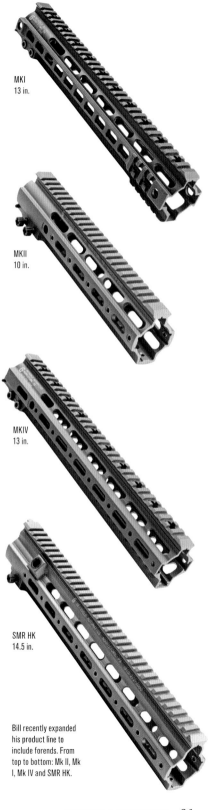

MKI
13 in.

MKII
10 in.

MKIV
13 in.

SMR HK
14.5 in.

Bill recently expanded his product line to include forends. From top to bottom: Mk II, Mk I, Mk IV and SMR HK.

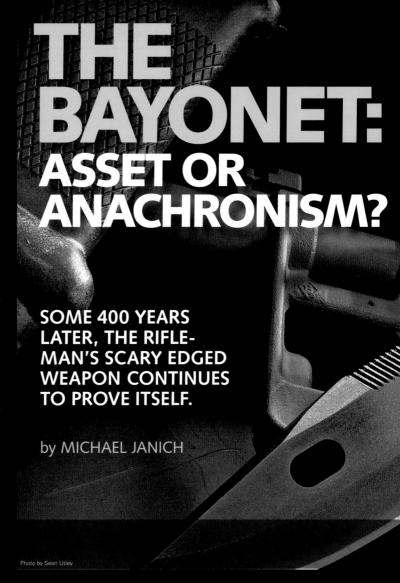

The bayonet was originally invented to allow soldiers to use their rifles as pikes if—or more likely, when—they either failed to fire or contact with an enemy was more imminent than a successful reload.

As firearms technology advanced and reliable multishot rifles became the norm, the actual need for the bayonet as a combat weapon steadily diminished. Bayonet training gradually became more of a means to instill fighting spirit and aggressiveness than a method of developing real combat skills.

Although well-designed and properly maintained bayonets can double as serviceable field knives, such tools are typically the exception to the rule. Many of the bayonets issued to modern soldiers are unsharpened and poorly designed, doing little to inspire their confidence. And to an infantryman conscious of every ounce of equipment he carries, a dull bayonet is much more likely to be left in a foot locker than carried in the field.

The true combat effectiveness of a bayonet is also directly affected by the design of the rifle to which it's attached. This is where the fascinating history of the AR-15/M16/M4 family of rifles takes another controversial turn.

When the M16 was officially adopted as the U.S. service rifle in 1964, it was paired with the M7 bayonet. The M7 was basically identical to the Korean War-era M4 bayonet that fit the M1 carbine. It shared the same blade design, injection-molded plastic grips and two-lever locking mechanism. The only real difference between the M7 and the M4 was that the guard of the M7 had a larger muzzle ring to fit over the flash-hider of the M16 rifle. As a side note, the M7 was also compatible with several other military rifles, primarily combat shotguns.

As a bayonet, the M7 was, unfortunately, very typical of its breed. As issued, it was normally not sharpened to a keen edge and its design, weight and balance made it a below-average field knife. Of greater concern, however, was the questionable logic of attaching a bayonet—any bayonet—to the M16 service rifle.

Anyone even remotely familiar with the controversy that surrounded the adoption of the M16 is well aware of the criticisms it faced. For the most part, these criticisms focused on its reliability and effectiveness as a firearm and the combat performance of the 5.56mm

THE BAYONET: ASSET OR ANACHRONISM?

SOME 400 YEARS LATER, THE RIFLE-MAN'S SCARY EDGED WEAPON CONTINUES TO PROVE ITSELF.

by MICHAEL JANICH

Photo by Sean Utley

cartridge. However, it is also interesting to note that many combat veterans disliked the M16 because it was not a suitable platform for the rigors of hardcore close combat, including bayonet tactics.

Classical bayonet tactics are much more involved than simply thrusting with it like a spear. They also include cutting techniques and a variety of striking patterns and combinations that involve the body and butt of the rifle. If you imagine a bayonet mounted to a classic battle rifle like an M1 Garand, you not only have a sharp spear blade backed by a "handle" with significant mass, you

also have a solid wood stock that can strike with both the power and structural strength of a baseball bat. It is also worth noting that your firing grip on the rifle is exactly the same as your grip for bayonet tactics. As a bayonet platform, it doesn't get much better than that.

If we contrast that to the structure of an M16, a number of shortcomings become immediately apparent. First, the overall weight and length of the rifle limit the effectiveness and penetration of bayonet thrusts. Its pistol-grip design also requires a significantly different firing grip that does not support a full range of bayonet tactics. To perform

The modern bayonet's virtues as a field knife may outweigh its value as an extension of the rifle.

most bayonet combinations, the operator must actually release his firing grip to grasp the small of the stock. But the most significant limitation of the M16 as a platform for bayonet tactics is the construction of its buttstock. Injection molded from plastic, the M16's buttstock does not have the weight or impact resilience to support the full-power butt strokes that figure so prominently in classical bayonet technique. More important, since the buffer assembly of the rifle is actually enclosed within the buttstock, any significant damage to the buttstock could actually render the action inoperable.

Although it seemed clear that the M16 was not a good platform for a bayonet, the M7 nevertheless remained in service throughout the Vietnam War and even after the U.S. Army discontinued mandatory bayonet training for soldiers in 1973. The M7 had a 6¾-inch blade ground from 1095 carbon steel. In addition to its primary edge, it had a three-inch sharpened false edge to increase penetration and theoretically support cuts with the back of the blade. Its injection-molded black plastic grips were textured, but their ergonomics left a lot to be desired. All metal parts of the M7, including the blade, cross guard

and locking mechanism, had a gray Parkerized finish.

Over the years, the M7 was manufactured by a number of different companies, but the primary sources for it were Bauer Ord Company, Colt and the Ontario Knife Company, which still produces it today. More than 3 million M7 bayonets have been manufactured and can be found with two variations of its M8 fiberglass sheath: one with a traditional belt loop and the M8A1 with a wire hanger for attachment to the grommets of military pistol belts.

The U.S. Marine Corps still engages in bayonet training as a method of instilling the warrior mindset.

The U.S. Army's M9 bayonet was introduced almost 25 years ago and when locked into its sheath, becomes a field wire cutter.

The U.S. military did not consider bayonets and bayonet training high priority after Vietnam. However, it did acknowledge the need for a serviceable field knife. It also decided that it should be capable of providing multiple functions—including that of a bayonet. The ultimate result of that thought process was the M9 Multi-Purpose Bayonet System (MPBS).

Designed by Phrobis III Limited, a research and development firm in Oceanside, CA, the M9 was developed to serve as a bayonet for the M16 and M4 carbine and a full-service field/combat knife. Featuring a wider, stronger blade than the M7, its textured thermoplastic nylon handle was a significant improvement over the M7's plastic handle. The design also included a section of saw teeth on the spine of the blade that could be used to cut wood, aircraft fuselages and even light wire. Its unique scabbard featured a flat-blade screwdriver and a sharpening stone, as well as a stud that fits through a hole in the M9's blade to allow the entire assembly to function as a wire cutter.

Phrobis maintained the patent rights to the M9, but licensed its production to the Buck Knife Company, which produced the M9 from 1986 through the early 1990s. The first Buck-made M9s were issued by the U.S. Army in 1987, and later Buck also produced a version of the bayonet for the U.S. In 1992, the Lan Cay company won the government contract for the M9 and simplified the production process. The resulting bayonets maintained the original M9 design, but did not feature the same degree of fit and finish as the original Buck versions. In 1995, Lan Cay also changed the blade finish of the M9 from its original unfinished gray to a black oxide coating. Currently, the Ontario Knife Company is the official source of the M9.

The U.S. Marine Corps has a very strong tradition of bayonet training and in 2002 decided to issue its own distinctive bayonet for the M16/M4 platform. The USMC Multipurpose Bayonet (MB) officially replaced the Vietnam-era M7 and was designed to serve both as a bayonet and full-service field/fighting knife. Also known as the Ontario OKC3S, it is manufactured exclusively by the Ontario Knife Company and measures a formidable 13¼

inches overall. It features an eight-inch clip-point blade ground from 1095 tool steel. Reminiscent of the iconic Marine Ka-Bar fighting knife, it has a broad blade profile and sharpened false edge. It also adds a section of serrations at the heel of the blade and a handle molded from flexible thermoplastic elastomer.

The USMC MB includes a scabbard made from thermoplastic elastomer that reduces its noise signature. Configured for attachment to MOLLE/PALS webbing, it also has a quick-release system that allows it to be easily removed from its mounting position. A built-in sharpening rod in the back of the scabbard supports edge maintenance in the field and helps make the USMC MB one of the most versatile, functional bayonet systems ever fielded.

Bayonets such as the M9 and USMC MB are a significant improvement over the original M7. They also prove that with proper design and execution, a truly functional fighting knife/bayonet can be produced for issue to our troops. However, the question remains: Is the bayonet still a viable weapon on today's battlefield, especially considering the

The M16's original bayonet was the M7, a modified M1 Carbine blade.

platform offered by modern assault rifles and carbines? One answer to that question has been offered by British military units serving in the current conflicts in the Middle East.

According to an account compiled by the U.S. Urban Warfare Analysis Center: "On 21 May 2004, Mahdi militiamen engaged a convoy consisting of approximately 20 British troops from the Argyll and Sutherland Highlanders 55 miles north of Basra, Iraq. A squad from the Princess of Wales regiment came to their assistance. What started as an attack on a passing convoy ended with at least 35 militiamen dead and just three British troops wounded…

"…The battle began when over 100 Mahdi army fighters ambushed two unarmored vehicles transporting around 20 Argylls on the isolated Route Six highway near the southern city of Amarah. Ensconced in trenches along the road, the militiamen fired mortars, rocket propelled grenades and machine gun rounds. The vehicles stopped and British troops returned fire. The Mahdi barrage caused enough damage to force the troops to exit the vehicles. The soldiers quickly established a defensive perimeter and radioed for reinforcements from the main British base at Amarah, Camp Abu Naji. Reinforcements from the Princess of Wales' Royal Regiment assisted the Argyles in an offensive operation against the Mahdi militiamen. When ammunition ran low among the British troops, the decision was made to fix bayonets for a direct assault.

"The British soldiers charged across 600 feet of open ground toward enemy trenches. They engaged in intense hand-to-hand fighting with the militiamen. Despite being outnumbered and lacking ammunition, the Argylls and Princess of Wales troops routed the enemy. The British troops killed about 20 militiamen in the bayonet charge and between 28 and 35 overall. Only three British soldiers were injured. This incident marked the first time in 22 years that the British army used bayonets in action. The previous incident occurred during the Falklands War in 1982."

In 2008 and 2009, British forces in Afghanistan successfully turned the tides of at least two other battles with similar bayonet charges. Interestingly, the issue service rifle of the British forces, the L85A2, is a bullpup design that is even less suited to traditional bayonet tactics than the AR platform. Nevertheless, their boldness of action

Left: *Rifles equipped with a bayonet lug will almost always have a 22mm flash-hider or brake to allow for mounting. Below: The Corps' MB bayonet pays stylistic homage to the classic KA-BAR knife.*

Photo by Sean Utley

Photo courtesy of DoD

and willingness to employ cold steel at close quarters made all the difference in these incidents.

Given the recent battlefield successes of the British, it is impossible to completely dismiss the bayonet as a valid tool of modern warfare. After all, if something works, it works. However, it is probably more accurate to understand the bayonet as a very literal reflection of the fighting spirit of the man wielding it. In the words of Cpl. Brian Wood, a member of the Princess of Wales' Royal Regiment involved in the Basra bayonet charge, "I wanted to put the fear of God into the enemy. I could see some dead bodies and eight blokes, some scrambling for their rifles. I've never seen such a look of fear in anyone's eyes before. I'm over six feet; I was covered in sweat, angry, red in the face, charging in with a bayonet and screaming my head off. You would be scared, too."

State-of-the-art bayonets designed to double as functional field knives definitely have a place in the kits of modern soldiers. And when backed with proper fighting spirit and determination, they remain a force to be reckoned with on today's battlefield.

Recruits at Parris Island battle with pugil sticks under the watchful eye of a close-combat instructor. As recently as 2009, British troops re-validated the bayonet with charges in Afghanistan.

Photo courtesy of DoD

BACKUP AR SIGHTS

Now that we have micro optics, will iron sights go the way of the ramrod?

BY **WAYNE VAN ZWOLL** | PHOTOS BY **MIKE ANSCHUETZ**

The AR-15 and its military counterpart, the M16, have generated more press in the last couple of years than any traditional sporting rifle. In part that's because AR-style rifles are so versatile—though they didn't start out that way.

Designed by Eugene Stoner, the original rifle in 5.56 NATO had little to recommend it for big-game hunting or National Match target events. In southeast Asia, the M16 drew plaudits and expletives. Improvements endeared it to law enforcement agencies. From LE lockers it jumped, in auto-loading form, to the civilian market. Cartridges such as the 6.8 Remington and .30 Remington AR added ballistic muscle.

Longer, heavier barrels and the Picatinny rail that appeared three decades ago on the M16 suit these powerful rifles to big-game hunting. At the same time, AR-15s have been configured for close-

quarters use. Carbine barrels and myriad attachments for front-end rails appeal to gadgeteers. The AR's presence on television, its rapid rate of fire and relatively cheap ammo—plus almost limitless combinations of aftermarket parts—have hiked its profile among people with only casual interest in guns.

After a half-century of development, the AR-15 has all but given up its iron sights. Most civilian versions are flattops with rails—a design feature that appeared with the A4 in time for the Marines to initiate it in Operation Iraqi Freedom. Now the U.S. Marines carry M16s equipped with ACOG sights,

Photo courtesy of DoD

First issued by the U.S. Marine Corps, the ACOG was quickly adopted by the Army after extended engagement ranges in Afghanistan pointed to the need for a magnified combat sight. It is one of the most durable, versatile combat optics ever devised.

RED DOTS

Optical sights boost the reach and precision of the soldier or Marine who is equipped with an M4 or M16. The ACOG, or Advanced Combat Optical Gunsight, comes from Trijicon. The Michigan firm has manufactured more than a half million of these compact riflescopes with the signature fiber optic tendril snaking around the short tube.

It complements a tritium element in the reticle for sure illumination without batteries. The U.S. Army has followed the Marine Corps in adopting Trijicon's 4x32 ACOG, the TA31RCO, and numerous models of the ACOG, from 1.5x16 to 6x48, are available to the civilian market.

Aimpoint is also known worldwide for its infantry optics. The U.S. Army has used the M68 since 1997. This classic, nonmagnified, 30mm-tube model employs a two-minute illuminated dot and a parallax-free lens system that has long distinguished Aimpoint optics. All of our armed forces have used Aimpoints, to include the M68 Close Combat Optic (CCO).

The M68 CCO manufactured by Aimpoint offers big advantages over traditional iron sights at close and intermediate ranges. Hundreds of thousands have been issued to troops in Iraq and Afghanistan.

HISTORY

The Rock River rifle sitting with me at my desk carries iron sights, the familiar A2 configuration. The A2-style rear aperture is certainly an improvement over the original set-up that began serving U.S. troops in Vietnam.

"The original M16 rifle issued to the Air Force, then to the Army and Marines, had several problems," observes David Fortier, contributor for Inter-Media Outdoors. "Some of the original M16 problems experienced in the field got immediate attention.

Others were addressed in an overhaul program led by the Marines in the early '80s." The new M16A2 featured a heavier barrel forward of the handguard and faster rifling twist to stabilize the SS109 62-grain bullet in the Belgian M855/856 cartridge. Full-auto fire gave way to a three-round-burst option (an M16A3 variation with full-auto capability was issued to specific forces and units). The stock was lengthened, then strengthened by the use of new DuPont Zytel polymers. Changes in the flash suppressor, handguard, grip and buttplate, plus the addition of a case deflector, improved the rifle's function. The A2 sights showed a shift in thinking about iron sights in combat.

The M16A1 rifle featured a dual-aperture rear sight on a pivoting base. The apertures were of the same diameter, but one had a slightly taller stem. Marked "L," it was to be used for shooting between 300 and 600 meters. The unmarked aperture served for closer shots. To adjust windage, you pressed a bullet tip into one of five detents in a small drum on the right-hand side of the sight. Elevation changes came by way of the front sight, a round post. It also had five bullet-tip detents. Rotating the post on its threaded stem moved it up and down.

The M16A2 rifle arrived with a square post for a front sight. This helped to reduce errors caused by

Photo courtesy of DoD

The M16's original iron sights were pretty lacking and were replaced on the A2 rifle fielded in the 1980s. Improved apertures and adjustments allowed Marine Corps recruits to accurately engage targets out to 500 yards.

light reflecting from the side of the curved surface. The ability to use a bullet to adjust front sight elevation remained, but now the post featured four detents. The rear sight was modified to incorporate a finger dial for windage adjustment. The two apertures in the L-shaped pivot piece were of different sizes, 2mm and 7mm, the latter for low-light engagements. Unlike the A1, the A2 apertures were engineered to deliver the same sightline, with no change in elevation.

"The Marines were largely responsible for the A2 sights," Fortier tells me. "Their training calls for shooting to 500 yards. And recruits are taught to adjust their sights for accurate long-range fire. The Army has traditionally trained its infantry at ranges to 300 yards, and it hews to a

While high-tech optics are now standard issue on flattop rifles, troops are still issued and practice with iron sights, should their primary optic fail in combat.

25-yard zero, admonishing the troops not to adjust their sights after zeroing." He adds that the knockdown targets in the Army's basic marksmanship drills show only gross errors in elevation.

Adoption of the newest M4 variant invited the use of many new sighting options. The MIL-STD 1913 Picatinny rail still accepts the traditional carry handle that's now detachable. Only now, soldiers are afforded red dots, magnified optics and folding backup sights.

The Army issues a folding backup sight from Knight's Armament Company with most M4s. Of course, the rail also accommodates MIL-SPEC scope rings. It is the most significant development in the AR-15/M16 rifle since the early 1960s, when a chrome-plated chamber and modified buffer system were introduced to address problems with jamming in combat experienced when ammunition issued to troops

with ball powders gummed up the M16 after long strings of fire.

THE IRON ADVANTAGE

The overwhelming preference for AR-style rifles with flattop uppers among the hunting fraternity mirrors the near universal use of optical sights by military units and law enforcement agencies. Practice with a scope or red dot sight gives any shooter faster, more precise aim than with iron sights. Still, iron sights can be both quick and accurate. Like many competitive shooters, I've used iron sights on paper targets out to 600 yards, and they've helped me drill dozens of one-hole five-shot groups at 50. Rifles with iron sights have brought me deer and bear, elk, pronghorn, caribou, mountain sheep and a half dozen species of African game at ranges from 15 feet to 180 yards.

Iron sights have several advantages over optics. They can deliver almost as much precision on big targets, but at lower cost with less weight, bulk and complexity. Irons designed for hard use remain less vulnerable to damage than optical sights, which is not the same as saying they're more rugged. The Trijicon, Aimpoint and even the Leupold Mark 4 CQ/T and Prismatic sights have proven themselves tough in battle.

DISADVANTAGES

Optics on ARs project higher above the barrel's bore line than iron sights,

Traditional iron sights weigh little and do not rely on batteries. As soldiers have equipped their rifles with optics like this Leupold Mark 4 CQ/T and other equipment, it has added weight and significantly changed the way the rifle handles.

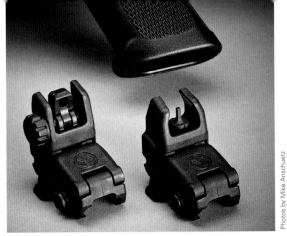

Backup iron sights are no longer just made of iron. Polymer pioneer Magpul has produced its own backup sights, mostly made of polymer, and they have proven extremely popular with civilian, military and law enforcement shooters.

so they get bumped more often. And, unfortunately, optics are commonly used as a quick carry handle for the AR when nothing else is as easy to grab. A durable glass sight shouldn't fail you, but damage to a rifle's iron sights is even less likely.

The weight of an optic on an AR doesn't necessarily make the rifle burdensome. A reflex-style red dot sight such as the Trijicon RMR weighs less than two ounces (I also appreciate its compact footprint). Battle-ready sights are heavier. The 4x32 ACOG scales 10 ounces, the Leupold Prismatic 12. At 17½ ounces, the Leupold's CQ/T adds 15 percent

The Trijicon RMR weighs less than two ounces and can be paired with a magnified optic, acting as a close-range sight for CQB.

to the rifle's weight. The seven-ounce Aimpoint boosts it little more than a set of irons. As important as the sum of ounces, however, is their distribution. Sighting gear sits well above your hands, especially on an AR. As the proportion of rifle weight above bore-line increases—as the center of gravity rises—the rifle becomes more awkward and slower to aim. Consider the lively feel of a traditional shotgun. No sights here. The shotgun's weight is carefully distributed, with most low between your hands, so it responds instantly. There's proper mass in the muzzle to settle a jerky mount, just enough to keep the barrel moving smoothly onto and with the target.

In profile, the AR is a radical departure from battle rifles of the past. The Krag and the Springfield had plenty of steel below bore-line and very little above. The M1 Garand and M14 wore their gas systems under the barrel. Like their predecessors, they used .30-caliber ammunition that added substantial weight to the magazine when it was full. In contrast, most issued AR rifles carry a gas tube above the barrel. The M16A1 and A2 feature integral carrying handles with the upper receiver. Sights are necessarily tall, both to clear the gas tube and handle and to deliver comfortable aim from a severely straight, thick stock. The buffer spring assembly on

direct-impingement ARs requires a tubular wrist in line with the bore. There's no way to get your cheek low enough to look down the barrel.

Still, iron sights make sense on many configurations of ARs. The Army-issued backup iron sight from KAC has a rail-grabbing base and is meant to be installed on the first (rearmost) rail notch. It "provides a backup capability effective out to at least 600 yards." To clear standard optics, the fold-down aperture can be left in the stowed position. It features the A2 windage adjustment.

THE AFTERMARKET

Today, there are so many choices in terms of a backup iron sight system. In most cases, these systems share similar principles to the M16A2 sight system in that they usually offer some type of windage and elevation adjustment. However, each new offering usually brings a unique approach to rear sight aperatures or a quick-access fold down/flip up capability.

XS offers its similar CSAT combat sight, with dual-aperture pivot, large and small. The latter has a square notch cut into the aperture rim for a more open view of the target and ability to quickly aim when the small aperture is in place. Thumbknobs let you attach the CSAT from XS Sight Systems without the use of tools (though they're also slotted).

Critics of the dual-aperture design allege that the small hole is too small, the big one too big. Proper aperture size depends on the target, the front sight, available light and, most significant, placement of the shooter's eye. In prone competition, I use a tiny aperture. My position puts my eye very close to the sight. The black bullseye on manila paper finds the aperture's center naturally. That sight would be a poor choice for the field, where the target is rarely as well defined and where shadows and mottled backgrounds reduce contrast. While I crawl the stock on hunting rifles, my eye stays far enough back to permit recoil. A seven-pound .30-'06 compresses eye relief suddenly and to a greater degree than my 13-pound .22-caliber prone rifle. Consequently, a bigger aperture makes sense.

I'm also conscious of the steel in the ring around apertures. It seems to me that ring thickness on hunting and battle sights, and on those for home defense, should equal the diameter of the aperture. Too much steel on the outside obscures more target than necessary. Too little ring becomes invisible in dim light.

The open notch on the CSAT might appeal to shooters who think the AK-47 open sight is superior to the AR's dual aperture. Designed in the aftermath of WWII and with an eye to Soviet combat on the Eastern Front, the AK-47 emphasizes reliability and fast shooting at modest ranges. Open-sight aim is a bit faster for inexperienced shooters because it can be done sloppily, with adequate precision for urgent close-range encounters. The contention that an open sight allows you to keep both eyes open is flawed, as it presumes you can't do that with an aperture or, for that matter, an optical sight. You can. For me, open sights are the

The Dueck Defense offset iron sights sit at a 45-degree angle to the rifle's primary optic. The operator simply has to tilt his rifle over to access the sights, a fast and simple arrangement.

most difficult to master with both eyes open. And they're easiest to misalign. An M16 front sight held .1 inch off center in the rear will cause a miss of five feet at 300 yards.

A square black post, or a blade that appears as a black post, is arguably the best front option when the target is a black disk. Not so for targets of varying shapes, colors and contrast in challenging light.

Unlike traditional sights on sporting rifles, AR front sights typically have protective ears. These can slow your aim if your eye doesn't come immediately into line with the sight axis. Differences in the profiles of ears and post can help you distinguish them quickly. A slant to the ears does, too.

Sight radius matters. A longer radius means more precision. The AR design puts the front sight at the gas block, not up front where it would better help you shoot accurately. Long barrels add sight radius.

AR barrels fitted with a front sight all but mandate that you at least carry a rear sight—zeroed, of course. Optical sight permitting, you're best served with the rear sight in place, where it offers an aiming option as quickly as you can pluck the glass. Of course, if your eyes are sharp and you're willing to practice a bit with irons, dispensing with optical sights altogether has much to recommend it. Your rifle will weigh less, point faster and better endure the bumps of field duty.

Troy Industries makes one of the most popular sets of BUIS on the market, and quite a few custom firearms manufacturers logo the sights as aftermarket parts to match their rifles, such as these from DPMS and Spikes Tactical.

APERTURE SIGHTS

DON'T NEGLECT THE BUIS.

BY SGM KYLE LAMB (RET.)
PHOTOS BY RICHARD KING

NOT A LOT OF THOUGHT IS PUT

EVEN THOUGH MANY SHOOTERS HAVE THEM MOUNTED AS BACKUP IRON SIGHTS (BUIS), I HAVE A FEW MORE USES AND THOUGHTS ON THIS PARTICULAR PIECE OF KIT.

As a shooting instructor, I prefer training shooters who have a solid understanding of the use of aperture sights on the carbine when they arrive. If not, they require additional training to get the needed know-how when it comes to running this type of sight, even to the point of understanding how to adjust the sight itself.

With most optics this is simple. Grab the dial and twist in the direction the little up or right arrow tells you to. This moves the impact of your bullet in that direction. With aperture sights it isn't always as easy. If you are planning to move the rear sight, you must move it the direction you want to move the bullet. The front sight is just the opposite. If you are hitting low, the front sight must go down to move the point of hold up, which in turn will move the bullet strike up. Hopefully, this makes things really confusing. Simply move the front sight the opposite direction you would like the impact to move.

WHY APERTURE SIGHTS
OVER OPTICS?

So why would you want iron sights in this day of modern optic technology? First and foremost would be their durability. You won't wonder if you break a sight if the rifle receives a few tough knocks. BUIS are another story. I prefer a sight that is heavy duty and can be locked in the up position. I don't want to look for sights and find that they are no longer in a position that is useable or, worse yet, start shooting and not get the

desired results. Second, irons don't require batteries. This is important if the choice of carbine is for home defense. Aperture sights are perfect for this type of setup — no need for bells and whistles when you are planning to shoot no more than 20 yards.

Even if you decide to simply have BUIS surrounding your red dot sight, always confirm that they are correctly zeroed for the same range as the red dot. With beginning shooters, I generally dial in the iron sights, then simply dial the red dot to the irons. For more experienced shooters working on an abbreviated timeline, it is just the opposite.

SIGHTS ON THE SAME PLANE

If you use iron sights, you will normally see a difference in the centering of the aperture circle. Elevation adjustments were built into military sights to allow the soldier to simply flip from the large aperture, which was designed for zero to 200 meters, to the smaller aperture for longer ranges. I don't necessarily follow this rule — I prefer to have the centers of the circle be on the same plane. This allows me to use the small aperture to zero at a specific meter line, usually 50, and be back on at 160 meters. Most say 50/200, but I have found that isn't necessarily the true distance. The smaller aperture will help to refine your sight picture and shoot much better groups.

FRONT SIGHT UP

One of the strange uses for BUIS is the utilization of the front as an aiming aid in an emergency. I always leave my front sight in the up position when shooting a red dot sight, which allows me to use the red dot as a large aperture and the front sight as a reference. This isn't perfect, but in a toe-to-toe encounter it will get the job done.

THE TECHNIQUE I USE AT CQB DISTANCE IS TO FLIP THE REAR SIGHT HALFWAY BETWEEN THE TWO APERTURES.

ELIMINATING PARALLAX

I also prefer to have the BUIS co-witness with the red dot sight. If possible, I try to rest the dot on the front sight during my zeroing procedure. I do not leave the rear sight up, only the front. This will help to maintain a better stock-to-cheek weld as well as eliminate parallax. A simplified explanation of parallax would be the movement of your group on the target as you move your head around behind the red dot optic. Once I contort into a compromised shooting position, I can return the dot to the top of the front sight to help get good hits. Many manufacturers build optic mounts that put the iron sights in the bottom third of your red dot glass. I don't care for this at all. It is much better to have the dot co-witnessed, and parallax is just one of the reasons.

GO HALFWAY

If speed is key at close distances, occasionally the large aperture is still not big enough. The technique I use at CQB distance is to flip the rear sight halfway between the two apertures. This allows you to look over the rear sight but still have a reference that allows for hostage-saving accuracy. It isn't the perfect solution, and you still have to maintain a hold-off of around 2½ inches to hit where you intend. You definitely should give this a try the next time you head to the range.

Photos by Richard King

Regardless of aperture type, sight alignment is achieved by centering the tip of the front sight post vertically and horizontally in the rear sight aperture.

DI-OPTIC SIGHTS

I thought the Di-Optic sights were a new way to spin a product for sales when I first saw them at the Troy Industries booth at the SHOT Show several years ago. Of course, I had to try some just to see what the deal was. Contrary to gimmicks, they work. The great improvement is the ability to have a reference to ensure that you are centered. A round hole is great, but the sides of the diamond help to drive your eye even more precisely to the center. This sight type will also help if you are trying to make small holdover corrections.

FULL-TIME APERTURE SIGHTS

If you do decide to run iron sights full-time, I would highly recommend two things: Get a good pair of nonflip-up sights, and ensure they have tritium. Solid sights will be better in the long run, and the tritium will help you to see your sights in even the darkest of situations. Of course, even if you do choose to use the irons, I would still employ a flashlight, but tritium will nevertheless help when you least expect it. I prefer to have tritium all around, not just on the front sight. This is costly, but it will pay you back tenfold if you have to put the rifle in action against the boogey man.

WHY WORRY?

As an experienced shooter, you shouldn't worry about the use of iron sights on your carbine. If you have reliable optics, the chances of using the BUIS for a real situation are very slim. The problem is that there *is* a slim chance, and Mr. Murphy loves low percentages of failure. He will be there standing with a smile on his face as your optic goes south. It is also important to work on true marksmanship fundamentals, and iron sights will tighten your fundamentals tremendously. Give it a try the next time you hit the range.

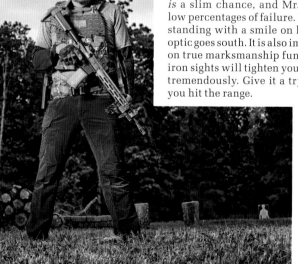

WHERE TO **ZERO** YOUR APERTURE SIGHT?

Since I prefer to co-witness my BUIS with my red dot optic, it's easy to remember the holds since they are the same for all sighting systems.

But what is truly the best distance to zero the iron sights on your carbine, and why?

I prefer to zero at 50 meters, as this setup will allow me to have the following rises and drops. Here is what happens if I am shooting M855, military Green Tip ammunition, which has a 62-grain bullet. With the 50-meter zero, I will be 1.11 inches high at 100 meters. This is such a small amount of deviation that you will never notice when shooting quickly. As the bullet passes 150 meters, you will be .66 inch high. Most of us can't see this difference either. As we continue downrange, we will be 1½ inches low at 200 meters — still nothing to worry about. At 300 meters our bullet will impact 12.27 inches low, which is significant but could be much worse.

Some would recommend the 25-meter zero, but I will have to disagree. If you zero at 25 meters, you will hit 2.1 inches high at 50 meters and 5½ inches high at 100 meters. This is significant and will not be an easy shot to hold. If you have only a head visible, you will have to go against common sense and hold low, which doesn't seem to work too well for me. Holding between the eyes will result in a round going over the head of the threat. At 200 meters you are seven inches high, and at 300 meters you are still three-quarters of an inch high. This is a great zero if all of your targets pop up at 300 meters, but for shorter distances the 25/300-meter zero isn't intuitive.

You have to make the decision, check your ammunition's ballistics and make an educated choice.

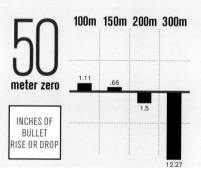

50 meter zero

| | 100m | 150m | 200m | 300m |

1.11   .66   1.5   12.27

INCHES OF BULLET RISE OR DROP

JOHN PAUL OF JP ENTERPRISES EXPLAINS THE DIF

THE **DOCTOR** IS IN

BY SGM KYLE LAMB (RET.)
PHOTOS BY MIKE ANSCHUETZ

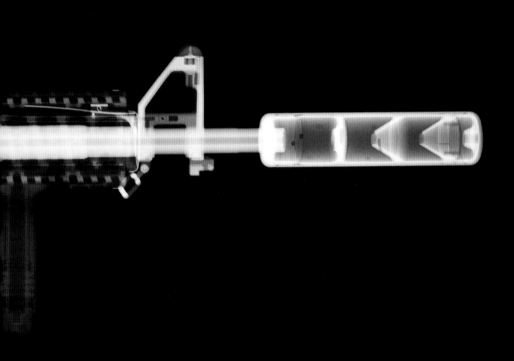

RENCE BETWEEN 5.56 NATO AND .223 REMINGTON.

So what is the difference between 5.56x45mm and .223 Rem.? And does it really matter? In order to answer these questions, I called the man I refer to as "The Doctor." John Paul is the brain behind JP Enterprises, a Minnesota-based firearms company that produces some of the most accurate and reliable ARs on the planet. Being the mad scientist that he is, I had to hire a local kid to translate John Paul's technical language into something a knuckle dragger like me could understand.

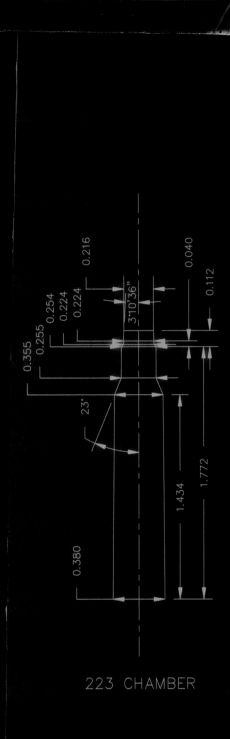

223 CHAMBER

JUST THOUSANDTHS OF AN INCH

The difference is in the throat or leade of the chamber. The throat is the distance from the chamber in your rifle to the lands or rifling in your barrel. When the bullet is still sitting in the case, how far the start of the rifling is from that chamber is the throat measurement. This is not a scientific explanation, just enough to make you a little more dangerous at the coffee shop when the subject of chambers comes up in conversation.

When Sporting Arms and Ammunition Manufacturers' Institute (SAAMI) specified the throat length for .223 Remington ammunition, it was spec'd at .085 inch. The leade in the 5.56 NATO cartridge is .162 inch, which equates to .077 inch more leade than the .223 Remington — almost twice the leade for the NATO cartridge. But does this difference really matter?

SAFETY

The down and dirty is this: You are normally safe to fire .223 Remington in the 5.56 NATO chambers, but the opposite may not always be true. If you decide to use 5.56 NATO ammo in your .223, you may also encounter pressure issues with the NATO round — not necessarily a good idea. The issue may be caused by the decreased throat length as well as the (sometimes) Mil-Spec versus SAAMI load you may encounter when using military surplus ammunition. The bottom line is that Mil-Spec ammo may run a bit hotter.

"A good example of this is the use of M193 military ammunition in a tight chamber such as the .223 Remington," says John Paul. "This particular ammo is finicky in hot weather, to say the least. Blown primers are the norm when this ammo is used in 5.56 NATO chambers, and the problem is only exacerbated when used in .223 Remington chambers."

RELIABILITY

Using 5.56 ammunition in a .223 carbine may also degrade your rifle's reliability. Excessive pressures coupled with ammunition that is just too long can have severe effects on overall reliability. Though you may see degradation in reliability, safety should not be an issue.

ACCURACY

If you have messed around with different loads trying to develop the tackdriver that you desire, you will already know that having your bullet close to the rifling is a part of the accuracy equation. It's not the only variable, but an important one to consider. This is one of the reasons 5.56 NATO-chambered carbines are not known for the greatest accuracy. They will definitely achieve acceptable accuracy for the combat marksman, but you will never achieve quarter-MOA groups with a 5.56 NATO chamber while firing .223 Remington ammunition. This is not to be an alarmist. I prefer 5.56 chambers over .223 in the carbines I use. They will hold the groups I require for realistic combat accuracy.

AMMUNITION AVAILABILITY

I like to shoot — a lot. So I need as much ammo as I can get my hands on to maintain proficiency with my AR platforms. I have had much better luck when my carbines have 1:7- or 1:8-inch twist and chrome- or Melonite-lined barrels with 5.56 NATO chambers. If you really want to get slick, you can follow the prescription The Doctor

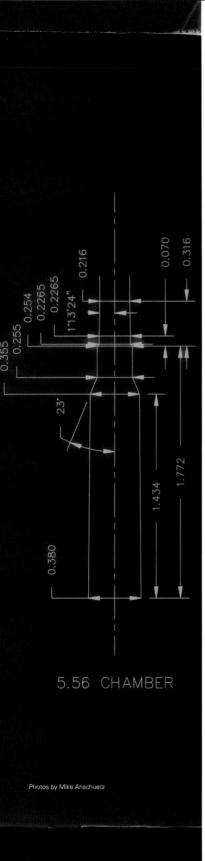

5.56 CHAMBER

recommends. Doctor Johnny Paul at JP Enterprise uses .223 Wylde chambers. The .223 Wylde is a great trade-off that's exceptionally reliable and incredibly accurate. JP's Wylde chambers have a leade that is a compromise of the two that lowers pressure concerns yet offers sufficient accuracy.

WHAT TWIST?

Another tidbit of info while we are on the subject of barrels: Some folks say twist rate of a carbine barrel doesn't really matter. With this I will whole-heartedly disagree. If you want to shoot heavier bullets in the 70- to 77-grain category, you will be much better served using a 1:7- or 1:8-twist barrel. Slower twist rates such as the 1:9 are fine if you are prairie dog hunting, but for big and heavy bullets, the quicker twist performs much better.

Actually, it's the length, not the weight that determines what the twist rate must be, but the two are usually closely related so it's not often an issue. For some of the new solid-type projectiles with no lead core, the length will determine the twist rate required, and faster twists rates may be needed for lighter bullets. In other words, you probably will not experience positive results with a 70-grain solid-copper bullet in a 1:9-twist barrel, even though a lead-core bullet of the same weight will shoot fine. The manufacturers will usually state the recommended twist rate for their component bullets right on the boxes.

At one time, AR-type rifles came with a 1:12 twist rate. This was largely due to the fact that the .223 Remington cartridge was designed with only light bullets up to 55 grains. These lightweights would stabilize at that slower rate of twist. Many people think that a faster-twist barrel will not shoot light bullets accurately and they will be "overstabilized." This is a myth. You can't overstabilize a bullet, but you can spin a lighter bullet so fast that it disintegrates from the centrifugal force once it leaves the muzzle. If this happens, you'll notice a gray streak leaving your muzzle toward the intended target, but no impact on the target. The bullet will vaporize if it can't handle the RPM.

The fact is that lighter bullets, even down to 50 grains, will shoot very accurately out of fast-twist barrels such as a 1:8 as long as they are constructed to take the higher RPM. So why not go with a rate that will shoot the broadest range of ammunition? It just makes sense. This should also explain why the U.S. military chose the 1:7 twist for its M4.

UNDETECTABLE

You can't see the difference in the .223 Remington and the 5.56 NATO chamber. You have to trust the manufacturer from whom you purchase your firearm to know and truly specify the correct chamber on the barrel you are using. You also have to trust the manufacturer on the twist rate, although this is something you can check.

Don't lose sleep over it. Just try to keep your gun safe full of every chamber available to fit ammo availability. Those are Doctor's orders.

Thanks to John Paul at JP Enterprises for his help with this article.

BIG BOOMERS

BY PATRICK SWEENEY

LEUPOLD

ON YOUR

AR

Say what?

The magazine sticks out on the left side of the Safety Harbor Firearms' SHTF-50 upper. And while it feeds fine, it can feel in the way.

From the bench, any .50 is going to be a handful. When the full-up weight is just under 20 pounds, things can get interesting.

It is in the nature of compromises that you have to give up something in order to get something. No matter how you try, or how good an attorney you hire, you simply cannot get around the Thermodynamic Laws. To launch really big bullets at impressive velocities takes a honkin' big gun, with mass and length, and cost.

One really big thing you have to resign yourself to when you decide you want to get into the really big bore is cost—the cost in ammo, bought or reloaded; the cost of size; and the cost of weight. One way you can trim the latter two is to give up on an all-steel, .50 BMG-dedicated blaster and use a conversion. A .50 BMG-specific rifle will probably tip the scales at 30 pounds and over six thousand dollars for a semi and 25 pounds and more than twenty-five hundred dollars for a bolt gun.

The most common conversion (actually, the only one I think is even possible) is to use a .50 BMG-chambered upper on your AR-15 lower. If anyone has made one for the AR-10-size receivers, I haven't heard of it, but I'd bet someone is working on it. All other rifles need not apply.

The process is simple. The new upper has a pair of attachment lugs, corresponding to the lugs on the upper of an AR-15. You push your assembly pins, remove your AR upper (5.56, 6.5, whatever it might be) and then install your .50 BMG upper and press the pin across. Violá! Instant .50 BMG rifle.

There are drawbacks, however. First of all, this is not going to be a self-loading rifle. Even if there were some way to attach a magazine (most are single-shots), the buffer weight and spring on your AR are hopelessly inadequate to handle the recoil of a reciprocating .50 BMG bolt. So your big .50 will be a bolt action. Also, it will probably be a single-shot, as the AR magazine well can't handle the .50 BMG, for obvious reasons. It is

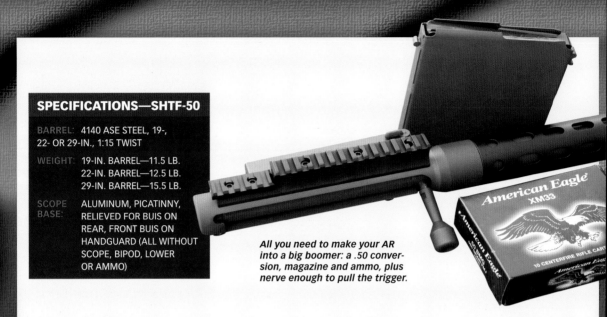

All you need to make your AR into a big boomer: a .50 conversion, magazine and ammo, plus nerve enough to pull the trigger.

entirely possible to design a replacement upper with its own magazine, a side-mount like a Sten gun on steroids, but that starts to make the rifle a lot more bulky and heavy, and the plus of magazine feed is probably more than offset by the size and weight.

Last is recoil. Your AR lower probably doesn't weigh much more than three pounds (if it does, you really should consider just how much gear you have bolted to it), and the full weight of the .50 BMG upper on your AR would be too light for comfortable shooting without a muzzlebrake. In fact, it would be hazardous to shoot such a lightweight .50, so your upper will have to have a muzzlebrake on it. Something big, effective, noisy and "blasty." You will not make any friends at the gun club shooting it, especially if your club has gone to the effort of putting a cover over the firing line. All that effort to keep the sun and rain off just makes the experience that much more miserable for those shooting around you.

As our exemplar, we'll be looking at the Safety Harbor

Firearms conversion of a .50 BMG onto an AR lower, called the SHTF-50. Not because I've tested them all and found the Safety Harbor to be the one for me (oh dear God no, I'm not going to test-fire every single .50 extant), but having looked over a few, I found the Safety Harbor offering to be an interesting and solid model to use as our test gun.

Safety Harbor offers the SHTF-50 in three different barrel lengths, 18, 22 and 29 inches. The barrels are made 4140 steel with a 1:15 twist, normal for the Big Fifty. The bolt is a two-lugged design, with the head made from 4340 steel and the bolt body from 4130, while the receiver is machined from 4130. In addition to the two locking lugs, the bolt handle nestles in a slot cut in the receiver, acting as a safety lug. On top is an aluminum scope mount (iron sights on a .50 BMG, unless it is an M2HB, would be an affectation) where you can bolt on the scope of your choice. My suggestion: something stout enough to handle the recoil you and your rifle

The magazine is stoutly made and feeds each round easily.

On the SHTF-50, everything is big and built for use, from the hefty bolt to the long bolt handle for better leverage in working the action.

will soon be experiencing. Now, if you want to put on iron sights, the scope mount is relieved for them and the front of the handguard has rails for a sight. Knock yourself out.

Unlike similar conversions, the Safety Harbor model offers a five-round magazine. The magazine and its housing look quite sturdy and able to survive incidents that you probably couldn't, like being run over by a car or truck. The magazine locks in place in a very interesting manner. The locking lever is in front; pivot to open. The lug on the magazine goes into a slot in the mag housing to the rear, then you lever and press the magazine into place. Once there, you close the locking lever. Why this way? First of all, it is simple and sturdy. Second, the recoil forces are not going to unseat the magazine, in fact, they'll act to keep it in place.

The barrel has a muzzlebrake on the end, and it is quite a ferocious-looking thing. With four slots on each side and internal baffles to scavenge more gas, it looks up to the task. Which is good, because there is a lot of recoil to deal with.

The scope mount is correct for height over the bore, and I was able to clamp a LaRue mount, with my Leupold 3-9X tactical scope on, without a problem. I had a goodly supply of Federal XM33 .50 BMG ammunition on hand, so it was time to lash everything together and get shooting.

That's where the compromises started kicking in. You see, you are not going to be able to swap an AR lower back and forth between your 5.56 upper and your .50 BMG upper. At least not without some work. First up, you'll have to install a hammer assembly with a stronger spring to drive the firing pin with greater force. The primers on .50 BMG ammunition are not like normal primers. They are meant for use in a machine gun, so they require a sharp blow to get their attention. Therefore, Safety Harbor includes a new hammer and

spring for use with the upper. Your drop-in match trigger unit, the one you use to shoot small groups? Won't work. Well, it might, but then again it might not set off the primers. Also, the access slot machined in the bolt, providing clearance to the firing pin, is machined to begin cocking the hammer.

Second, the bolt will not work (the upper won't even close) if you have your bolt hold-open installed. You'll have to remove that to use the AR lower. Finally, the buffer and spring serve no purpose, so you have to remove them, too. And as a final step, you have to take out the buffer retainer plunger. You see, the bolt on the .50 conversion has a slot to provide access to the firing pin to the hammer of the lower. If you try to work the bolt of the conversion with the buffer retainer plunger in place, it simply causes problems and jerky bolt work. Save yourself the hassle; take it out.

Which means we're essentially using an AR lower as a dedicated lower on which to place the .50 conversion.

Once done, the system is large and heavy. The base weight of the 22 inch upper is 15½ pounds. Add the bipod (a wise investment, and Safety Harbor makes a good one), scope, lower and ammo and you have a system that gets really close to 20 pounds. Any other extras you add simply pile on the weight. A 22-inch barrel may not seem like muc. After all, you've packed a 20-inch AR-15, right? Well, the 15 pounds you're adding is all out front. And

The bolt handle rides down into this slot, acting as a safety lug for the big .50 boomer.

You can see the brake and the internal gas scavengers.

WHAT IS IT LIKE TO SHOOT? AWESOME. TERRIFYING. SERIOUS WORK.

the side-mounted magazine makes it kind of awkward to handle while walking or stalking.

And let me be clear here: I'm not picking on Safety Harbor on this. All .50 BMG conversions are going to suffer the same things. It is the nature of compromise.

You will be glad for that weight when you go to fire your conversion. Even as effective as the comp is—and the weight helps—you are dealing with major energy. To give you an idea, a handgun for IPSC competition has to generate Major Power Factor. Weight times velocity has to equal or exceed 165,000. A .30-'06 will generate 450,000; a duck load in a 12 3-inch magnum will produce 600,000. Your XM33 round, fired from the SHTF-50, generates a power factor of 1,680,000. That is correct—three magnum duck or geese loads all at once. Ten .45 ACP or even more .223 rounds at once.

What is it like to shoot? Awesome. Terrifying. Serious work. Even with the weight and the comp, if you do not have a secure hold and a solid cheekweld, you will be seeing stars. The comp? I'm sure it helps, as it blew a notebook off the shooting bench next to mine the first

time I fired the rifle. You will not make any friends while shooting this rifle, especially if your club has a covered firing line. Federal makes good ammo, and I'm a more than passable shot. But with the recoil and backblast magnified by the covered line (my club rules don't allow firing except on the line), I was doing good to shoot two MOA. I'm sure I can do better, but that will have to wait until I can get out from under a roof.

The effect of this recoil on your lower receiver is as yet unknown. Theoretically, the recoil of the big Browning

If you want to shoot well, you need to see well. And the recoil of a .50 BMG is going to punish your scope. Buy a good one such as this Leupold or you'll be buying another one later.

ACCURACY & CHRONOGRAPH DATA

Load	Bullet Weight (gr.)	Muzzle Velocity (fps)	Standard Deviation	Average Group (in.)
Federal XM33FMJ	660	2,459	23.7	2.0

Chronograph was a PACT MkIV, two-foot screen spacing. Centered 25 feet from the muzzle. Velocity is the average of five rounds; group accuracy is the average of four five-shot groups.

Left: You'll have to remove the bolt holdopen in order to install your .50 BMG conversion. Right: Save the parts. If you decide you've had enough recoil, you'll need them when you go back to 5.56.

should simply reduce your AR lower to a pile of aluminum scrap. After all, each shot is the equivalent of launching more than a dozen 5.56 bullets simultaneously. You'd think that it would only take a few shots to scrap your receiver, but that is not the case. I have not heard of receivers busting right and left. So obviously, the wear is not as great as first thought might indicate. Still, there has to be accelerated wear, so keep an eye on your lower. And if you do bust one, figure out if the cost to fix it is worth it. I figure that at the price of .50 ammo, you will have gone through many times the cost of a new receiver (even if it expires relatively quickly) in your ammo costs, so unless you live someplace where lowers are restricted, you might just look on an AR lower as a consumable. Shoot it until it is too worn to be useful, then scrap and replace it. How much of a problem is this? Simple: Will the first guy who has to do that let us know? We have yet to hear of anyone doing so, so I figure it isn't much of a problem.

Now that we've given you all the reasons you should not have bought that upper, let's look at the good stuff. First, power. The basic .50 BMG loading is a 660-grain bullet (there are loadings with heavier bullets) moving along at 2,700 fps. Now, the XM33 specs assume the ammo is fired from an M2HB, which has a 45-inch barrel. By using one-half the length (the sample I had is a 22-inch barrel), you're going to lose velocity, but not a lot, as the .50 BMG has never been subject to powder improvements. And why should it have been? It has been plenty good enough for nearly a century now. Which leads us

Do it right; use the correct tool. Don't knarf your rifle just because you want to convert it "right now."

to the second part: There are no SAAMI specs on the .50 BMG, so proceed carefully.

As much fun (and work) shooting this has been, I would restrict my shooting to either current-production Federal XM33, Hornady A-Max or reloads I've loaded that match those specs or come in a bit behind them. This is not a cartridge you try to magnumize, and saving money by buying surplus ammo from Carjackistan is false economy.

But if you have the room (there isn't much that's more fun than busting big rocks a kilometer away) and the wallet, this is a gun that will make all your friends jealous. Just be ready for the recoil.

Left: Shooting a .50 BMG rifle is work. Don't go into it lightly, and don't shoot so much you build bad habits. Right: This is a nice start, and with a bit more practice this rifle should be shooting one-hole groups.

THE TRUTH
About Carbon Fiber Barrels

by GREG RODRIGUEZ

Carbon fiber-wrapped barrels are nothing new. Gunsmiths have been building carbon-barreled guns for a long time now. Many 'smiths have made bold claims about the accuracy and heat dissipation of their tubes, and some of those makers have built an excellent reputation. But mixed reports on the accuracy and heat dissipation of carbon barrels from several knowledgeable friends have always left me lukewarm on the hi-tech tubes.

The past couple of years, an increasing number of positive reports about carbon-wrapped barrels from top shooters I know and respect made me reconsider these barrels. Many of the carbon-barrel shooters I know

swear by ABS Barrels and gunmaker KK Jense of Jense Precision. Last year I called KK to discuss carbon fiber-wrapped barrels. I ended up ordering a new rifle and learning a whole lot about carbon barrels in the process.

WHY CARBON?

Carbon barrel proponents cite three reasons for their hi-tech barrel selection: light weight, accuracy and heat dissipation (plus all the benefits that come with reduced heat, such as longer barrel life). There is no arguing the weight savings; carbon fiber-wrapped barrels are significantly lighter than steel tubes. On average, a carbon fiber-wrapped barrel will weigh about half of the weight of a steel barrel with the same profile, but the difference is greater on heavier tubes and less on gas gun barrels. For example, a 26-inch, seven-contour barrel will weigh 4½ pounds less than a conventional barrel with a similar profile. On an

Rodriguez testing his carbon carbine with the Nikon M-223 scope and Surefire suppressor.

Above: The author's high-dollar Franken-gun was put together by KK Jense of Jense Precision. It ran flawlessly and balanced beautifully, even with its Surefire suppressor mounted. Right: Adams Arms' piston system has three-positions, including a suppressed mode. The Surefire muzzlebrake is a good one. It is also the attachment point for Rodriguez's Surefire suppressor.

AR carbine barrel, the weight difference is only about a half-pound, but the difference goes up fast on thicker precision rifle barrels. That is a significant savings, especially for a gun that will be carried a lot.

Regardless of whether you use your gun for hunting, defense or target shooting, pinpoint precision is important. Stiff, heavy barrels are renowned for their accuracy. Thanks to their proprietary carbon wrapping process later, ABS's barrels are also stiff, but they use a combination of accelerating and decelerating helices to manage the harmonics of the barrel. The helices increase the frequency and decrease the amplitude of the vibrations, resulting in less barrel movement and increased accuracy.

Their increased accuracy is also a result of the fact that ABS's carbon-wrapped barrels dissipate heat much faster than conventional tubes. In fact, they dissipate heat close to 400 percent faster than steel barrels. Less heat means barrels last longer and foul less.

ABS's carbon-wrapped barrels also dissipate heat more evenly. Steel barrels tend to heat up excessively at the chamber, which can accelerate wear. Tests have proven that ABS's barrels tend to dissipate heat more evenly along the barrel's length, with the chamber and muzzle having a minimal temperature differential after just four or five minutes. The chambers of steel barrels, on the other hand, are much hotter than the muzzle for a half-hour.

WHY ABS?

Early carbon fiber barrels (and many still in production) consisted of a carbon sleeve around a thin steel barrel. The sleeve is held in place by tension. It sounds like a great idea until you consider the science. Steel expands when heated. Carbon fiber contracts when subjected to

that same heat. As a result, the amount of tension changes as the barrel heats, which leads to very erratic accuracy.

The design of those old sleeved barrels presented another problem in that the sleeve actually acts as an insulator and holds in heat rather than allowing it to dissipate. The problem was further exacerbated by the fact that those early barrels were made with the wrong type of carbon fiber. Heat travels along those PAN (Polymerized Acrylonitrile) fibers rather than across them, because PAN fibers don't allow heat to cross from fiber to fiber. In addition, most PAN fibers do not even have the same capacity to carry heat as steel, so in many cases steel would be a more effective choice than those poor-quality carbon-wrapped barrels.

Another problem is that the thermal transfer coefficients of

Above: Rodriguez tested this carbon-barreled, direct-gas upper from Jense Precision on a custom lower by George Gardner at GA Precision. Right: These two carbon-wrapped barrels weigh about ⅔ less than steel barrels with similar profiles.

PAN-type carbon fiber material and steel are also very close, while the application actually begs for a bigger difference for maximum heat dissipation. Those two factors combine to make the older-style carbon barrels abysmal failures in the heat-dissipation department. In fact, they actually increase heat and accelerate barrel wear.

ABS's barrels are wrapped with a fiber that is the result of the polymerization of coal tar pitch. The pitch-type fiber is extremely stiff and has a much higher coefficient of thermal conduction than PAN fibers. Like all carbon fiber, it contracts when heated, but ABS found a way to deal with that, too. Carbon fiber tends to conduct heat along its fibers. ABS had to come up with a radical new approach to get heat to cross from fiber to fiber and keep the carbon fiber from acting as an insulator. To do it, it came up with a patented method of tuning its barrels by manipulating the helix angle of the carbon fiber wrap, a special filament winding technique and a duplex fiber con-

tent, which is a very high grade of PAN and pitch-type fibers.

That's a whole lot of fancy words to describe a barrel, but the technology really works. ABS's barrels have been proven to dissipate heat and increase barrel life by up to three or four times. That means the tube on your favorite mega-velocity barrel burner could last 4,000 to 5,000 rounds rather than 1,000 to 1,500 rounds.

Some shooters I know questioned the durability of carbon-wrapped barrels. Though I don't have enough experience with them to say definitively, the folks I've talked to who use them say they are just as rugged as a steel tube. One private contractor who has extensive combat experience with carbon barrels on multiple combat tours states that durability is not an issue.

A SOLID FOUNDATION

ABS doesn't actually make barrels. Instead, it orders high-quality barrels from top makers such as Satern, Krieger, Rock Creek, Broughton

and Classic Barrel & Gunworks in the length, caliber and rate of twist of your choice. Barrels are turned down to the correct diameter by the original maker and then carbon-wrapped by the folks at ABS.

Long before I owned an ABS-barreled gun, I owned custom rifles with barrels from all the above makers. All shoot phenomenally well on their respective custom sticks, and their bores are smooth and easy to clean. In short, they exhibit all the characteristics a fine custom tube should.

THE CARBON CARBINE

Other than a few groups here and there with Christiansen Arms rifles belonging to hunting clients, I didn't have much experience with carbon-wrapped barrels until I received my tricked-out carbon-barreled AR-15 from Jense Precision.

I chose to go the carbon route on the AR-15 solely because of the weight. I usually shoot my ARs suppressed, and sticking a can on the end of the gun makes it awfully muzzle-heavy. I assumed that the carbon-wrapped Rock barrel I chose would help me keep down the weight so the suppressed rifle would balance better and be easier to tote. It worked, but the lightweight tube didn't just shave a few pounds off the package. The custom carbine balances way better—with or without the can—than a steel-barreled AR.

I had a bunch of parts on hand, so I had KK use them for my build. The upper and lower receivers are from DPMS. The lower parts kit is from Rock River, the trigger is a Geissele part, and the bolt and bolt carrier are Wilson Combat parts. The grip and UBR stock are from Magpul, and the 12-inch Light Rail is from Daniel Defense. A Surefire muzzlebrake keeps me locked on target for fast follow-up shots and allows me to quickly attach or remove my Surefire sound suppressor.

Though it is a little heavier than traditional carbine stocks, I chose the Magpul UBR stock because I felt the increased weight would balance out the suppressor-equipped AR. It worked, because the gun points effortlessly with the can on it.

Because heat is the enemy when it comes to reliability and accuracy, I asked KK to build my carbine as a piston gun. KK suggested I use one of Adams Arms' rifle-length piston kits. Though the Adams piston system adds a bit of weight to the package, the ultra-reliable, three-position piston system has a proven reputation for relentless reliability. And, like all piston systems, the Adams kit vents gases and unburned powder out the front of the gun, rather than back into the action. Consequently, piston guns run cleaner and cooler than traditional, direct gas guns. Not surprisingly, they are more reliable and keep running longer than traditional ARs.

I installed Troy Industries' excellent flip-up iron sights just in case, then mounted two optical sighting systems. For CQB work, I installed Aimpoint's little Micro dot sight on a LaRue mount. The tiny little sight weighs next to nothing, but its four-MOA red dot makes it easy to make accurate hits in a hurry.

My hunting and knock-about optic is Nikon's 2-8x35 M-223 riflescope in one of Nikon's M-223 mounts. The compact sight is fairly light and has a wide field of view, but its eight-power top end allows me to really reach out there. Its Rapid Action Turrets allow me to dial up a dead-on hold out to 600 yards with the hi-tech carbine.

PUTTING IT TO THE TEST

Lacking any scientific way of comparing my new carbon carbine to a conventional steel-barreled AR, I decided to just shoot the hell out of it, one of KK's direct gas guns with a carbon fiber barrel and two of my steel-barreled ARs—a direct gas gun and another maker's piston gun—in sort of a side-by-side comparison. While my impressions are purely subjective, I have an awful lot of time behind various ARs and feel they are worth detailing here.

First, when it comes to weight and balance, the carbon fiber-barreled carbines won hands down. They are a solid 1½ to two pounds lighter than similarly equipped steel-barreled guns, which makes them easier to wield during extended firing sessions. They also come right on target fast and easy. In multiple-target training scenarios, I didn't catch myself seriously overswinging targets with them like I tend to do with my other ARs, especially those with a suppressor attached.

When it comes to heat dissipation, the carbon guns won easily. To test it, my training partners and I fired four 30-round magazines through each gun as fast as we could pull the trigger. Immediately

afterward, the carbon-wrapped barrels were slightly cooler than the steel barrels, but the difference was very pronounced after just five minutes. Ten minutes in, the difference was still significant.

THE BOTTOM LINE

My test was far from scientific, but there is no doubt that carbon-wrapped barrels dissipate heat much faster than steel tubes. I believe the piston operating system also contributed to those lower overall temperatures. The reduced heat and decreased fouling combine to make a carbon-barreled piston gun the ne plus ultra when it comes to reliability.

Reduced heat and barrel fouling also contribute to increased accuracy and longer barrel life. How much? Well, it would take a lot more time, instruments and study than I have to devote to the subject. However, common sense dictates that carbon-wrapped barrels that dissipate heat almost 400 percent faster than steel tubes will last longer and maintain their accuracy better than steel tubes of the same quality. Field reports from several top shooters I know who have extensive experience with carbon-wrapped barrels back this up.

Carbon-wrapped barrels by top makers such as ABS are expensive. Are they worth it? Well, probably not if your AR is just a safe queen. But if your job requires you to carry a carbine in harm's way, the light weight, heat dissipation and increased accuracy of a carbon fiber-wrapped barrel make the hi-tech tubes well worth the price.

PART IV
TESTS & TACTICS

MIRROR IMAGE

LIFE FROM THE OTHER SIDE OF THE GUN.

BECAUSE OF A VISION problem I've had in my right eye since birth, I shoot rifles left-handed, but I'm actually right-handed. I've learned to deal with the continual disappointment that comes with shooting long guns in a right-hand-dominated world, so shooting an AR left-handed has never presented itself as a problem to me.

Even before the case deflector became standard equipment on the AR platform, I don't recall any ill effects from shooting one without it. Occasionally, some hot gases and unburned powder will hit me on the right cheek, and if the AR is well oiled I'll get sludge on my face and shooting glasses. But none of this has ever interfered with my shooting. It's just a little annoying.

This is all fine until you throw a suppressor in the mix. Years ago I bought a Gemtech G5. I placed it on an AR and proceeded to shoot. About five rounds into it I knew there was a problem, one that would render that suppressor useless, in my opinion. All the back pressure from the can was blowing the gases from the receiver directly into my face. I couldn't breathe while shooting suppressed. I tried adjusting my head and cheekweld, but nothing worked.

TEXT AND PHOTOS BY Sean Utley

My suppressor sat dormant for quite some time until I came across the Robinson XCR. It has a gas system that's adjustable and has a suppressor setting. I thought this was the fix for my problem, but in the end it wouldn't be. I still had the same issue, which obviously is not due to any malfunction . It's just that I was shooting wrong-handed.

THE AR'S PROBLEMS FOR LEFTIES

I got my first Stag "lefty" upper about four years ago. It was a frankengun of sorts. It was when the piston gun craze was moving ahead full tilt, and I wanted one badly so that I could run a suppressor and experience the benefits of a clean-running AR. I acquired an Adams Arms (AA) piston kit, then called Samson Manufacturing Corp. and they milled out the rail that would go on the Stag left-hand upper so that the AA piston would fit underneath. Stag put it all together. The barrel was then cut to just 10½ inches. Yes, it was a lot of work, but definitely worth it. I finally had a lefty piston gun early in the game, so I took the setup to a three-day carbine class at Tactical Defense Ohio. There wasn't one issue after roughly 900 rounds (85 percent of which was suppressed).

Since then I've had several left-hand ARs made, and it seems that more and more people are shooting left-handed. Many have expressed frustrations with right-hand guns, particularly in the AR platform. My advice has always been to get a left-hand upper. But the upper itself is only part of the solution. There's the lower as well, where obviously most of the gun manipulation takes place. Your trigger engagement, mag release and safety activation/deactivation all take place on the lower.

Then there's the charging handle. The disconnect latch is not easily operated by a left-handed

A true left-hand rifle will permit its operator access to controls like the magazine release with the fire-control hand. That's only going to happen with an ambidextrous mag release.

individual. The only thing on the AR that is remotely lefty friendly is the bolt release that can be depressed by your trigger finger (if it's strong enough) following the insertion of a magazine once the bolt is locked to the rear. But for the most part, we southpaws no longer have to settle for second-rate ergonomics. With countless new accessories for the AR-type rifle, we can finally set up our guns to run neck-and-neck with the righties of this world. (Not to forget the fact that many manufacturers are sending guns out of the factory as ambidextrous setups.)

A couple of my law enforcement friends have expressed that they don't want to get a lefty rifle or have a lefty setup because if for some reason they have to pick up another officer's gun to use it, they want familiarity. That's a valid point. But if you pick up someone else's gun, who's to say that he won't have a setup that is different from yours? What if he has an optic and that optic has a different reticle, eye relief or zoom? Will his light or laser be on the same side? Will the activation switch be in the same place? When was the last time you set up your gun and thought *I'm going to run my light here so that when I drop my weapon it will be easier for someone else to operate it*? We simply can't rely on someone else's gun to be to our personal specs. That's why it's good to have excellent general weapons familiarity. This can be achieved by handling and shooting several different guns as often as you can. Take notes of the features and how they operate.

In a training environment, wouldn't it be more effective to be able to tell your trainees to disengage the safety with a strong-hand thumb or use a trigger finger to depress the magazine release, no matter what hand is most dominant for the shooter? With a properly set-up, ambidextrous carbine, the motions are mirrored on either side of the rifle. This should mean adaptation happens quicker also. Trigger finger does this, support hand does that. And I haven't encountered any training as

This build features a free-float quad rail system made for Stag Arms by Samson manufacturing.

of late that didn't require us to shoot strong side and weak side, and be able to transition from side to side so that we can use cover and concealment properly. With effective training and a little extra time and effort, we can learn to run the AR-type rifle the same way with either hand.

BACK TO STAG

I spent three of five days attending the 2011 SHOT Show from a hotel room with food poisoning. But before the illness hit, I did get to spot Stag's 11½-inch short-barreled upper with a 1:7-twist barrel. It was good to see, as I could only get 1:9 barrels from Stag up until this point. In the past, I was having any barrel I purchased chopped down to SBR length. I wanted the ability to shoot the heavier 77 grain out of the shorter barrel for better projectile stability and effectiveness.

The crew at Stag were kind enough to send me one of its 11½-inch SBR-TL rifles for testing. It features a chrome-lined Delta-profile heavy barrel and M4 feed ramps. I must also note that Stag uses left-hand barrel extensions on their left-hand guns. As noted before, it is a 1:7 twist, stamped as such on the barrel just forward of the front sight with the letters "MP," denoting the magnetic particle testing. Surrounding the barrel is a free-floating, Samson Star-C quad rail. It's the same rail that I have on my early lefty piston gun. It's a solid, quality rail system.

The SBR-TL also sports an F-marked front sight. What's most awesome about this is that it also has a side sling swivel, located on the right side. Side sling mounts were always on the other side of the gun, so I've been running single-point slings for years because they were

This 11½-inch barrel utilizes a 1:7 twist and is topped off with SureFire's FH556-212A flash hider that serves this shorty as an adapter for a SureFire suppressor.

easier for my left-handedness. With the Stag side sling swivel in place I can now use a two-point sling properly, and that ejection port is no longer resting against my body. It's the little things that mean so much.

Stag also installed an A.R.M.S. #71L-R rear flip-up sight. The sight is polymer and spring loaded. It has two apertures: one for close-up work and the other for targets at distance. Simply flip up the secondary aperture in front of the first with your finger. Both apertures are notched on top so they can be used like pistol sights.

The bolt and bolt carrier are of course designed for left-hand operation. This particular model came with an M16 bolt carrier and, like the barrel, the bolt is marked as MP tested.

I run ambidextrous safeties on all of my ARs. I find it easier and more efficient to deactivate the safety with my left (strong hand) thumb on the right side of the gun, and to reactivate it with my index/trigger finger. It's lightning fast and requires minimal movement (even though I have pretty small hands). Some don't like ambi safeties, as the lever on the side opposite of the shooter's thumb can interfere with grip and safety actuation. This is particularly an issue if the shooter utilizes a high grip. I have never had that issue, but it is something to consider. It's for this reason that rifles from Stag Arms can be bought with a left-hand-only selector lever.

I WANT MORE

This left-hander's journey to the perfect AR

A left-handed shooter can appreciate the functionality of a charging handle release lever positioned on the right side, a left-hand selector and sling options opened up by the incorporated right-side sling attachment point.

setup has been years long, tiring and full of disappointments. I've spent lots of dough chasing down the next great part or accessory that was to make my rifle time faster and more efficient. And I still haven't found perfection. However, I believe that we lefties are closer than ever as our options continue to get better. There really is no reason for a left-hander to have to overly modify or learn some strange or contorted method of running an AR comfortably. Looking back, it wasn't the case even two to three years ago, but there are now several different brands of ambi charging handles, safety selectors and magazine releases available for the discerning shooter.

CHANGES IN SETUP

Once the Stag arrived, I made some changes to satisfy my personal tastes. I took off the standard pistol grip and replaced it with a Magpul MIAD. While I had the grip off, I also ditched the right-hand safety selector and replaced it with the Battle Arms Development ambidextrous Safety Selector (know as the "BAD-ASS"). In my humble opinion this is the best safety selector available. It comes with three different

Though the ejection port cover is simply inverted and flips up to open, a number of design changes to the bolt carrier group and lower have also got to be completed before an AR begins to favor a left-handed shooter. Consider what it takes Stag to engineer a left-hand brass deflector.

lever options allowing the shooter to customize it to his liking. There is a standard lever, a short lever and a thin lever. One might set up his gun like this: Place the standard lever on the side of the receiver where your thumb safety lever usually resides, but on the other side you can install the flat lever so there's less interference with your grip. I run the standard lever on the right side (strong thumb) and the short lever on the opposite side. This allows me to actuate the safety in the aforementioned thumb-off, forefinger-on manner. It allows great purchase on the levers. I have the BAD-ASS for my semiauto and full-auto receivers as well. Select fire is where I believe the ambi safety really begins to shine. Once you make the longish throw to AUTO, it can be awkward getting the selector back to Semi or SAFE. By using an ambi selector like the one from Battle Arms Development, you can easily move from Semi to Auto and back while using the forefinger and

thumb. With a little training it quickly becomes second nature. The BAD-ASS also features a stainless steel detent that allows the selector lever to move in an extremely smooth manner. It slips in and out of battery with a very positive click that can be felt and heard.

After installing the new grip and safety selector I added what has become a "must have" piece on my ARs: a Knight's Armament (KAC) ambidextrous magazine release. I installed my first one roughly three years ago and have been buying them ever since. Up until recently your only options for lefty-friendly mag releases were the Norgon and the KAC. What makes the Knight's so much better is the leverage you can get with its extended design. With the Norgon, if you had inserted a full magazine with the bolt closed, it was nearly impossible to eject that same full magazine. You'd have to push hard on the bottom of the magazine just to get the button to actuate. The Knight's has a long lever that extends back toward the shooter's hand and allows for much more leverage. I can pop out a fully loaded magazine pretty easily with this. I must note that the positioning of the lever is a bit awkward, as the optimal area to depress is closer to the shooter's hand and not as ergonomically situated as the standard button on the right side of the gun. A little time with it and you'll get past this. I must also note that during this writing I was sent a gun with a Troy ambi mag release already installed. After looking over the Troy approach, the first thing I did was insert a fully loaded mag (for me, 28 rounds) into the rifle on a closed bolt. I was pleasantly surprised when I put just a standard amount of pressure on the lever and the magazine popped free. In fact, it was easier than with the KAC release. And the design of the Troy allows the finger to actuate the release button much like you would if you were right-handed, using the standard right-hand mag release.

An ambi mag release is not a necessity, and depending on how you've been taught or trained, the standard AR magazine-release location is quite good for a left-handed shooter. If you practice the grab, release and pull method—throwing the magazine completely clear of the mag well with your right hand—then leave your mag release alone. It's simple to grab the magazine with your support hand while pressing the mag-release button with your thumb, then yanking the magazine clear. I'm always looking for that extra second, so I like to be able to have my hand already on a fresh magazine and on its way to the gun while letting the emptier magazine drop free (hopefully) on its own. Tomato, *tomahto*.

As far as the lower was concerned, that's all I did to this project—outside of swapping the M4 stock with a Vltor Enhanced Modstock (EMod) and adding the all-important ambi charging handle.

I've always used the Badger Ordnance out of habit. There are a couple of other brands worth noting, one being the Armadynamics ambi charging handle, and recently I've used the Troy version. I suggest you get your hands on each and figure out which one will fit your needs best. One thing I must communicate about the Armadynamics is that this handle is spring loaded, thus it relies on the bolt being forward to provide the resistance that allows it to unlatch from the upper receiver when you pull back on the charging handle. So if the bolt is locked in the rearward position and the charging handle is locked in its forward position, you have to press a small button on the left side of the handle to release the charging handle so it can be pulled rearward. It sounds confusing. In essence, if the bolt is open, you have to push a button while pulling on the charging handle to move it rearward. Much like a standard charging handle. The Troy is pretty straightforward with latches on both sides of the "T" in the handle. They work smoothly with no drama. Seems to be a solid design. I'm still partial to the BO, especially since they added the larger tactical latch to the right side of the handle. I remember when the large tactical latch came out for right-handers (which did nothing to help my situation). But a tactical latch for a lefty means that you can get a positive hold on the charging handle, using your support forefinger and thumb or even using the outside of the palm of your hand. It also allows you to get around that pesky forward assist that is completely in the way if you're running a right-handed upper. The first Badger handles had small latches that meant you had to grab them just right to charge the handle on a standard upper. The new larger latch means the forward assist is no longer a problem for us lefties. If you run a left-handed upper from Stag Arms, it's a nonissue because the forward assist will appear on the left side of the rifle.

OTHER GOODIES

Once the rifle was complete, I topped it off with a tan EOTech EXPS3. Optics are one of those things where you either like them or you don't. I've run the EOTech through lots of training, and I definitely like it. The reticle is the best available for my shooting, and I appreciate the viewing area it provides.

This shorty left project was complete with the quick attachment of a SureFire MINI suppressor. At just five inches in length and weighing two ounces less than a pound, this can not only provides significant sound suppression, but it does so without adding a lot of weight and length to the profile.

And last but not least, I needed a suppressor. It would be sinful to set up a compact lefty carbine without a suppressor (knowing full well that I wouldn't encounter any fouling in my face). The upper and lower fit on this Stag is extremely tight, so I wasn't concerned about gas pushing out between the fitments. I've never noticed an issue with gas even when fit wasn't as tight.

SureFire allowed me to evaluate the new MINI suppressor for a 5.56. My time with SureFire suppressors on this gun was pivotal. Hesitant at first, I went prone and shot round after round and noticed I wasn't getting gassed in the face. I assumed it was due to the prone position pulling my face away from the ejection port. But I also guessed it could be something inherent to the SureFire design.

The SureFire MINI is light, weighing just 14 ounces, and (as its name suggests) it's pretty short at five inches. Interestingly, a credit to its design is the fact that it only adds 2¾ inches to the length of your rifle. That's perfect for keeping an SBR, just that—an SBR. I hate having a short gun, then adding a six-inch suppressor, then having something as long as, or longer than, my initial starting point.

The Mini is attached to the Stag by way of SureFire's FH556-212A flash-hider adapter. Its method of attachment and detachment is excellent, and it's always easy to get the suppressor on and off. I even tested this by removing the can while it was still quite warm using only my bare hands. Because I didn't have to spend too much time fumbling with the attachment, I avoided any discomfort.

There are many benefits to having a suppressor on an SBR. The most obvious is the reduction in sound and muzzle flash. Short barrels are well known for their fire-spewing abilities and being louder than their 16-inch counterpart. The MINI helps bring all of this under control. And one of SureFire's claims to fame is its ability to provide a minimal and consistent zero shift when you use one of its products. I was able to see this first-hand with my initial testing of SureFire's suppressors last year, and in my own testing that claim would hold true.

SHOOTING

Black Hills' 77-grain BTHP was used for testing. Being a 1:7-twist gun, I figured this was the best choice. I only use the 77-grain for occasional shooting, as it's certainly expensive when compared with 55-grain projectiles. I compared these results by testing this configuration with 70-grain Barnes TSX BT bullets loaded by Silver State Armory. I had some magazines with 55-grain Privi as well, stuff that I use for training. I didn't have high hopes for its accuracy potential, but 55-grain ammo is what I shoot 97 percent of the time, so I thought I'd better try it.

My big mistake on that first range session was forgetting a magnified optic. When I got to the range all I had was an EOTech. Disappointed in myself, I fell back to the "run what you brung" school of thought, so the EOTech would be it. I settled on 50 yards to determine this rifle's accuracy potential, even though I regularly use such optics out to 200 yards on eight-inch steel targets. But I've never used one to do any real accuracy testing. That being said, I was surprised by how difficult it was to use the EOTech in this situation as I was trying to put the dot that resides in the center of the reticle directly on top of a red dot on the letter-size paper 50 yards away. I shot groups both suppressed and unsuppressed and was surprised by the results.

With the 77-grain Black Hills unsuppressed, the best I could muster was a 10-shot group with a 3.38-inch spread. Without the inevitable flier the spread was just under 2.81 inches. The 70-grain Silver State printed a 1.94-inch spread unsuppressed. Without the flier it was 1.38 inches. These results surprised me, as I was fully expecting the 77-grain load to yield the better result.

Next, I attached the SureFire MINI to see what changes would occur with the gun. The Black Hills 77 grain printed 2.63 inches at its widest spread. So the

The VltorMod was chosen by the author to replace the standard M4-type collapsible stock that arrived from Stag. The EMod is about one inch longer than the original Modstock, something considered to be a benefit when used on scoped rifles.

The standard charging handle on this project was exchanged with a left-hand tactical charging handle from Badger Ordnance for just $73.

group was indeed smaller, and the point of impact had not changed. The accuracy claims from SureFire are indeed true. During unsuppressed fire, this Stag liked the Silver State 70-grain load more than the 77 grain. It would hold true in the suppressed firing as well. A 1.88-inch spread resulted. Minus the flier, four shots fell into one inch. It's a very tight pattern, and the zero did not shift. The SureFire was only making things better. I'm certain that, revisiting this evaluation with a magnified optic, much better results could be obtained from both of these cartridges.

The 55-grain Privi is clearly not the best for this rifle. It printed a pattern averaging six inches. I shoot 55 grain almost all the time, and I try to save the heavier ammo for the times when I particularly need it. With precision guns I've always realized the importance of finding the right ammo. I never gave it much thought in these shorties, but after seeing the results of the testing I'll be paying more attention to what ammo I get for my SBRs. I won't assume that because it's heavier it'll be the best for the 1:7 twist.

Because I'm very aware of the quality ammo that Black Hills makes, I just had to verify that

it was indeed the rifle and ammo combo that wasn't providing the expected accuracy. My friend who was shooting with me brought along his own precision .223 bolt gun, sporting a 1:7 twist. As suspected, it's simply a case of this particular SBT-TL model liking the 70-grain Silver State ammo better. The bolt gun printed three shots of the Black Hills into one hole. It really didn't make the first hole larger; they simply all went in exactly the same place.

After the accuracy test, we proceeded with some function tests and fired a few magazines in AUTO mode. We encountered no malfunctions. I'd never shot a left-hand gun in full auto before, and I walked away from the range having loved it. My friend couldn't say the same, as he's right-handed. After one magazine through this SBR-TL, he'd had enough. The SureFire suppressor was attached, and he couldn't take the gas. Though I didn't say it out loud to him, all I could think was, *Welcome to life from the other side of the gun.*

SPECIFICATIONS
STAG ARMS SBR-TL

TYPE	Direct impingement, semiauto
CALIBER	5.56 NATO
CAPACITY	30 rds.
BARREL	11.5 in., 1:7 twist, chrome lined
OVERALL LENGTH	29.37 in. (collapsed)
WEIGHT	7 lbs., 2 oz.
GRIP	Magpul MIAD
STOCK	Vltor EMod
TRIGGER	Mil-Spec
SIGHTS	Elevation adj. A2 (front), Adj. A.R.M.S. #71L-R flip up (rear)
MSRP	$765 (upper), $300 (lower), $200 (Form 1 Tax Stamp)
MANUFACTURER	Stag Arms 860-229-9994 stagarms.com

The National Match course and other forms of position shooting can be modified to suit any marksmanship goal. The All Army competition is shot with issued rifles and ammunition while wearing standard uniforms and combat gear.

High-level Service Rifle competitors, military and civilian, typically make excellent instructors. This is one of the reasons competitive shooting programs began in the military.

The bullseye provides needed objectivity in ... proved marksmanship, as silhouettes on a p... up range fail to provide detailed feedback. ... bullseye doesn't test facets of tactical shoo... all the necessary fundamental skills are bet... drilled here.

BY JOHN BUOL

BULLSEYE FOR WARRIORS

High power as it relates to combat.

Why would anyone want to shoot at black dots? Every soldier justifying his lack of participation in conventional shooting has likely made that statement. For whatever reason, millions of troops have never attempted to test their marksmanship skills against a bullseye course. The honest ones, comfortable with their egos, will admit that they simply don't have the skills to shoot such a course well and aren't willing to put in the work. That's fine. I've never been on a golf course and will never shoot par.

The problem is that some soldiers try to convince others and themselves that this lack of participation and ability on such a course is fully acceptable because bullseye isn't "realistic." Fact is, conventional shooting is the best approach to developing superior marksmanship skills and is the original foundation of all firearms skill.

The explosion of mass-produced, yet accurate rifles in the 1880s made individual marksmanship training worthwhile. Despite this, such training was slow to catch on, as no prescribed system or standard existed. It was left to the whim of the unit commander. Influenced by civilian competition shooters, forward-thinking high-echelon leaders such as General Philip Sheridan, then U.S. Army chief of staff, began encouraging competitive shooting programs to find the best talent among the ranks. Competition shooting promoters William Church and George Wingate would publish material teaching their methods learned at matches, which evolved into the U.S. Army's first marksmanship manual. The formats used eventually became the National Match course created for the M1873 Trapdoor Springfield, the issue rifle of the day. Originally, this comprised three seven-round slow-fire strings shot at 200 yards standing, 300 yards kneeling and

600 yards prone. By 1892 the U.S. Army had adopted its first repeater, the Krag-Jorgensen rifle, and its first smokeless cartridge, the .30 Army (.30-40 Krag). This made rapid-fire practical, and a change to the course of fire was made. The slow-fire portion was mostly the same, with two stages of rapid fire added, each fired as two five-round strings. At 200, from standing, the time limit was 20 seconds per string, and at 300, from sitting or kneeling, the time limit was 30.

National Match shooting comprised range exercises originally developed to train skills with military-issue rifles and pistols. As shooters improved, match-grade versions were developed, providing new ideas and improvements for current-issue small arms. As event participants improve skills, accurized versions encourage further practice and development. These top shooters trained on accurate versions of issue service firearms typically make the best instructors. A recent example of this occurred during the mass mobilizations in 2004. There was a heightened demand for designated marksmen. However, personnel in charge of training soon

realized that they lacked the skill and know-how to provide it. High-level civilian service rifle competitors were recruited at a number of mobilization platforms to augment military instructors.

Formal competition has been the primary driving force behind nearly every shooting skill and many equipment developments even if most shooters, military and civilian, don't realize it. Service Rifle shooters competing in National Match Across-the-Course events need a rifle capable of one-minute accuracy at 600 yards. Since the dawn of smokeless propellant, this had been the domain of issue .30-caliber cartridges starting with the .30 Army (.30-40 Krag), and it was widely believed that the little .223 varmint round wouldn't be up to the task. This thinking prevailed for three decades, with

Designated marksman skills have been in high demand in-theater for the duration of the recent wars. Bullseye shooters developed and taught all the initial classes for this skill set.

Improvements found in the issue M16A2 service rifle, including the sights, float tube and better ammunition, can be traced directly to Service Rifle shooters.

In testing basic marksmanship skills, a simple aim point with an easily defined center point is all that's needed. The goal is to hit as close to that center point as possible with each shot. A series of concentric circles radiate from the middle, with the center point clearly designated by a central circle marked "X" and surrounded by the 10-ring. A shot anywhere in this area is deemed "perfect" and given a maximum value of 10 points. Shots landing farther away from this center in any direction are awarded less points, with each corresponding circle out worth one point less.

Evaluating the marksman's efforts is simplicity itself. Each bullet hole is worth the value assigned to the smallest scoring circle it touches. Tally up the earned points. Scoring points may seem a bit arbitrary, but it provides solid objectivity. The standard is clear—you either earn a certain number of points or you do not. To challenge marksmanship skills further, the target can be moved farther away, a smaller target can be substituted or a reduced time limit can be imposed. Bullseye targets are the best next step after sighting in. Once a zero has been established, it should be confirmed from position. The first rule of marksmanship is to learn to hold the gun the same way for each shot. How the rifle behaves in recoil will be different from each position, and this can affect shot placement. Add in possible variables caused by pressure applied to the fore-end, from the sling, etc. and the need for testing from realistic field shooting positions is apparent.

Bullseye targets also teach another lesson important in the field: Proper shot placement is more important than raw precision. Yes, shooting the tightest group possible is always the goal when zeroing

military rifle teams continuing to use M14s through the 1990s. Service Rifle teams finally began looking at ways to make the M16 work. While organized shooting events are clearly superior for developing higher-level marksmen, a number of the match modifications have trickled down into combat gear. Looking at the current M16 series, the A2 rear sight, free-float handguards and rails, and magazine-length 77-grain projectiles as used in Mk 262 ammunition were first developed to defeat the black dots.

The fact is, bullseye-type shooting is beneficial. We now take it for granted, but the basic bullseye target was an important step forward in testing marksmanship proficiency.

More than 150 years ago, shooting accuracy was often recorded by "string measure." Pegs were pounded in the bullet holes shot through the target's surface, and a string was wrapped around them, with the shortest string winning. It isn't hard to imagine how tedious it would be to score a target, and it was soon realized that a cleaner, faster system was needed. If you think about it, all the intricacies of marksmanship and the related equipment boil down to trying to put bullets in the same place, to hit the center of the intended target every time. Of course, arms and ammunition are only so accurate, and even the best-trained human operator is subject to a whole host of foibles, so some deviation is to be expected.

Even though support has dwindled over the years, all the services maintain competitive rifle teams. These teams can trace their history to the origins of marksmanship training in the military.

or position shooting, and a group that is abnormally large indicates a problem. However, true accuracy takes shot placement—how close the shot or groups hit from the intended point of impact—into account. A four-minute group centered around the intended point of impact (in and around the 10-ring) scores more points than a one-minute group in the wrong place (wide outside of the black), and this is true in the field, too.

Soldiers and most other gun owners fail to appreciate the virtue of bullseye shooting for practice and skill development. They see the use of specialized guns and gear and assume it can't help them. True, conventional shooting fails to address a number of issues critical to success afield. However, using silhouette targets, for practice or competition, should be viewed as a test of the raw marksmanship skills already developed. For exercising these most basic skills, the bullseye target has few peers.

REAL RELEVANCE

I'm sure there are a few self-appointed masters of tactical shooting who are scoffing by now. How could the bulls-

eye targets they perform so poorly on or maybe have never used possibly be tactical? Well, pull-ups, pushups and squats aren't tactical movements either, but they are useful exercises. Shooting bullseye is, too. Look at the NRA SR-3 target. The aiming black extends out to the 19-inch-wide eight-ring, the exact same width as a military E-type silhouette, and the 10-ring is seven inches, about the size of a human head. The outer five-ring spans a yard across, a bit smaller than a Double E-type target used to simulate an enemy fighting position or crew-served weapon. For National Match shooting, this target is engaged rapid fire, requiring the shooter to drop into prone from standing and shoot 10 rounds with a reload. The MR target is engaged at 600 yards and features an E-type-width nine-ring (18 inches) and a 36-inch bullseye. Top shooters rarely stray from the nine-ring, and clean targets (all shots inside the 12-inch 10-ring) are not uncommon. Tied scores at 600 yards are decided by the head-size X-ring. Remember, this is done with an accurized M16 and iron sights using only a sling for support. As you can see, bullseye target dimensions are not arbitrary. The

scoring rings represent sizes similar to targets engaged in the real world and/or are in even minute-of-angle increments to make sight adjustment easier.

Still not convinced? Let's look at what the current masters of mayhem are using for range exercises. Within the Department of Defense, the U.S. Marine Corps is one of the few bastions of marksmanship training. Both Marine rifle and pistol qualification courses still use round bullseyes for major portions of each Marine's assessment. Is the Marine Corps not tough enough for you? Consider the SFAUC (Special Forces Advanced Urban Combat) course. SF9661 is the CMMS (Combat Marksmanship) portion, and the first four days include practice and firing for record on NRA competition bullseye targets. The SOTIC (Special Operations Target Interdiction Course) teaches Special Forces sniper training and employment, and their methods are detailed in FM 3-05.222 (TC 31-32). Special forces snipers make use of National Match bullseye shooting, and their data book has space for scoring bullseye matches. The M24 sniper rifle includes Redfield

Top bullseye rifle shooters have shot perfect scores on the Army machine gun qualification course. It features timed pop-up silhouette targets out to 800 meters and is normally shot with a crew-served, tripod-mounted machine gun with 154 rounds of ammo. Good bullseye shooters have cleaned it with an issue rifle and less than one magazine.

Palma iron sights for this type of target shooting. Former operators-turned-trainers such as Kyle Lamb and Larry Vickers use bullseye targets in their training. As Vickers so eloquently puts it, "I am not here to give you what you want, I am here to give you what you need." Posers and pretenders aside, actual operators still conduct portions of their combat training on bullseye targets.

Now that you're convinced that bullseye might be better for your skills than you thought, how can you use it to your benefit? The obvious approach is to find organized events in your area and start attending. Borrowing wisdom from the infamous Japanese swordsman Miyamoto Musashi, find a path to follow and seek to learn as much as you can about that path. This includes knowing the tools, skills and knowledge of that path. If you desire to become a master of riflecraft, you must rigorously study the ways and tools of the rifleman. Competition provides such a path as well as guideposts, milestones and helpful, knowledgeable people in a no-BS environment to guide you on your journey.

If competition isn't in the cards for you (a damn shame and your loss if it's not), you can borrow ideas from bullseye shooters to improve rou-

Effective training can be conducted on scaled targets at short range. Even military qualification targets have an internal score ring and can be scored to reward better performance.

tine qualification. Even if stuck on a 25-meter range, slow-fire shooting from unsupported positions should be added. Prone unsupported and kneeling are required during regular qualification, and sitting and standing can be added. Once you're happy with your zero from sandbag-supported prone, try groups from these other positions. Improving this is the reason why bullseye shooting was invented in the first place. Rapid fire is also a component of bullseye shooting with 10-round time limits between 50 to 70 seconds, including time to get into position and reload midstring. This typically requires a firing rate of one shot every two or three seconds, which also happens to be a good rate for effective suppressive fire. Again, National Match competition is not an arbitrary game. Using U.S.

Army Alt C targets at 25 meters, load a five-round magazine and empty it on one target in 10 seconds. Any hit in the silhouette scores a point, and hits inside the four-centimeter circle score two. Consistently scoring 10 points per string means every shot is good enough to hit inside the black on the SR-3 target at 300 yards or hit an E-type silhouette at speed every time.

All high-level competition shooters with combat experience I know, have interviewed or have read about agree that competition shooting, including conventional bullseye-type competition, was directly beneficial to their fighting success. Let's face it, learning to shoot at a higher skill level while under pressure can only improve your ability to shoot under pressure. Only those who have never been involved in formal competition, or have fared poorly there, attempt to denigrate its value. Learn to shoot better on a bullseye target and you'll shoot better everywhere else.

Conventional shooting using bullseye targets formulated the first marksmanship training programs. The origins of this are still seen in U.S. Marine Corps qualifications.

BY **SGM KYLE E. LAMB** (RET.)

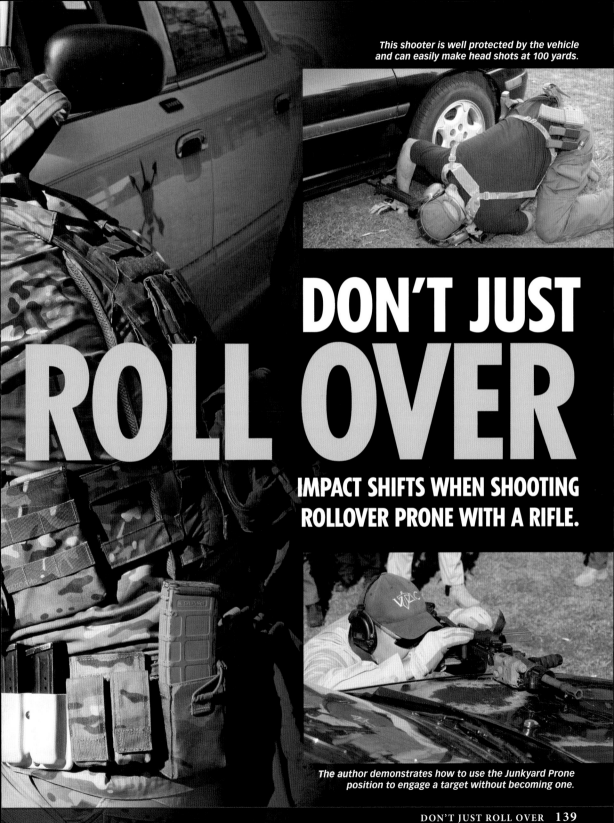

This shooter is well protected by the vehicle and can easily make head shots at 100 yards.

DON'T JUST ROLL OVER

IMPACT SHIFTS WHEN SHOOTING ROLLOVER PRONE WITH A RIFLE.

The author demonstrates how to use the Junkyard Prone position to engage a target without becoming one.

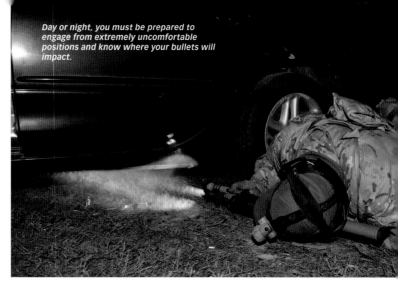
Day or night, you must be prepared to engage from extremely uncomfortable positions and know where your bullets will impact.

You encounter fire from the enemy; you take cover behind a low-slung vehicle; you prepare to engage the threat, or what little of him you can see.

As you crawl into position you realize the car is so low to the pavement that you will have to lay your carbine on its side to effectively see your sights and engage. So if this threat is at 100 yards, where will you hold to make an effective shot? What if that same threat is on the opposite side of the vehicle, only three yards from your position?

Every time I ask this simple question of our new students: "Where will the bullet impact from your point of aim when laying the carbine 90 degrees right or left?" I get several answers, most of them simply guesses.

If you fancy yourself a combat marksman, you must know where your rounds will impact at any given realistic distance. You must also know where the impact will be if you decide to shoot from a nonstandard position under a car or over the hood of a vehicle.

100 YARDS AND FARTHER

So what happens when the gun is canted left or right?

Let's start with a 90-degree cant to the right. That is, the carbine is laid on its right side, the sights being farthest to the right. Your line of sight will be a straight line, but the trajectory of the bullet will never be straight. It does not matter how hot the load you are shooting, you will have what some call a parabolic curve, which is the bullet's path or trajectory. With normal trajectory with the gun held in the standard position, the bullet will most times cross your line of sight twice. I prefer a 50-yard zero with my AR-type platforms, so this allows me to be roughly zeroed at 50 and 250. The bullet's trajectory crosses my line of sight at 50, rises above the line of sight and drops back across the line of sight again at 250, in a perfect world.

All this being said, where will that trajectory arc be carved when we lay the gun to the side?

Gravity will immediately start to affect the trajectory of the bullet, so if the carbine is laid on its right side, the bullet will definitely be dropping lower than normal. Remember, with your normal zero the bullet is rising because the barrel is pointed at a slight uphill angle. With the rifle on its side, there is no uphill, so to

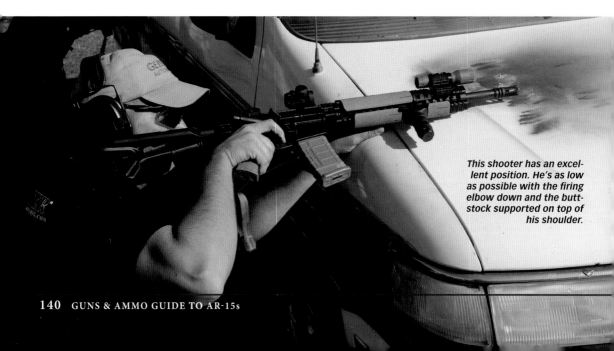
This shooter has an excellent position. He's as low as possible with the firing elbow down and the buttstock supported on top of his shoulder.

This target is the result of shooting at 100 yards using the Leupold CQBSS 1-8X scope and an ASYM 75-grain load. The impact is six inches off center and at a 45-degree angle from point of aim when shooting with the rifle laying on its right side.

Facing page, top left: This soldier drops into position. This may be the only option you have in certain scenarios. He's using the vertical grip hooked on his arm for recoil control. Top right: When it is time to shoot, where do you hold at three yards? Bottom: If you hold your sights between the threat's eyes, you will hit in the RED circle (bottom). If you hold on his mouth, you will hit right in the nasal cavity indicated by the BLUE circle. If you hit high on the skull in the RED circle, there's a chance that the bullet will skip off and not penetrate. Hitting in the nose is a better option.

speak. This simply means that you will see more bullet drop than you are accustomed to.

You also have to contend with the rise of the bullet. In the normal position, as stated before, the bullet is rising. This is because of the barrel pointing slightly up. Now we still have the barrel launching the bullet toward our line of sight, which happens to be to the right of the barrel instead of above the barrel. This will account for the bullet curving in a different and less desirable manner. That is, if you don't know where to hold.

WHAT'S THE RULE?

My rule is this. If the carbine is laid to the right, your bullet will impact low and right. If it's is laid to the left, the bullet will impact low and left. As a good starting point we normally see about eight inches at a 45-degree angle low and to the side you are laying the weapon on. This is if you are shooting from 100 yards. This isn't always true, so you should try this the next time you are on the range.

HIGH TO THE MAGAZINE SIDE

One of our students who struggled with this type of shooting finally had

enough and said, "Just aim high to the magazine side." This makes total sense, and I have used this in every class I teach so that shooters will immediately know where to hold. As I said earlier, test this theory on your own so you know where to hold for the different yardages at which you will need to shoot. When I am engaging targets at 50 yards and as close as 25 yards, I do not use any hold-off. You will have to judge this for yourself once you get on the range.

No matter the position, aim high to the magazine side when laying the carbine 90 degrees from your normal position and you should be good to go—that is, if you are at a distance over 75 yards.

EXTREME CLOSE RANGE

Oh, how simple this all seems, but wait. There is always more. If the distance is five yards and closer, where will the bullet impact? If you think it doesn't matter, you may be wrong—hopefully not dead wrong. As we shoot

These examples of two different positions from the same cover definitely drive home the point of using Junkyard Prone and knowing your hold-offs. Keep your head down, and quickly eliminate the threat.

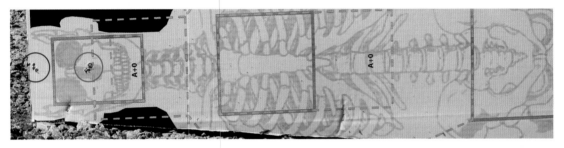

Staying as low as possible is key. Know where you need to hold, because you may not have time to analyze the situation.

This rifle is free of gadgets on the left side, allowing for it to be as close to cover as possible. This is something important to consider when setting up your rifle. Here you just see a VTAC Extreme Battle Rail and Light Mount.

at extreme close range the rounds will now impact in a straight line in the direction of the barrel from your line of sight, at least 2½ inches. This may not seem like a lot, but if only a portion of your target is exposed, you must pick the correct spot to hold your sights.

Aim where you need to aim, not where you want to hit.

So if I throw myself in the dirt and attempt to engage a threat with the gun laying on the right side, I will have bullets impacting at least 2½ inches to the left. Let me quickly

explain why this occurs. Sight offset from your barrel is normally at least 2½ inches with the standard M4 Carbine configuration. This will increase with most standard mounting options for red dot and magnified optics.

ELIMINATING PARALLAX

In this day and age it would seem that you need only point your rifle in the general direction of the target and let the high-speed, laser-guided, illuminated, variable, ranging, trajectory-compensating scopes take over, resulting in target lock reminiscent of a fighter pilot and his F-16. In other words, just fire and forget. Well, not so fast. Huge advancements have been made in the firearm optics industry over the last 20 years, but we still have to deal with small issues that may drive you crazy when trying to engage targets quickly from nonstandard positions.

What Is Parallax?

Parallax is the reticle of your scope aligned on a slightly different focal plane than where the target actually is. Imagine you have a target at 600 yards. Your scope thinks the target is at 100 yards, therefore the scope, shooter and firearm are all a bit confused. This confusion comes in the form of perceived wobble in your sights or slight sight movements when shifting your head and eye around behind your riflescope.

If you want to see parallax, set your scope on a table. Do not touch it. Pick out a target at 100 yards, and move your head around behind the scope. If the reticle moves on the target, you have parallax. If the reticle does not appear to move, pick out another target at a different distance and go through the procedure again.

Don't obstruct your dustcover when using the Roll Over positions, as this is a sure way to induce a stoppage.

Your scope may have one minute of parallax or one foot of parallax. This is something you need to know.

If you are using a sniper scope of any quality, it will have a knob located on the left side of the tube. This is used to dial the correct parallax setting into the scope. Most shooters call this the reticle focus knob, and in actuality, if every setting is correct your reticle will be in focus when parallax is adjusted. But truth be told, this knob is to adjust parallax.

You hear shooters and trainers talk about parallax; you hear manufacturers decree that their scope is parallax free. Last time I checked, the Hubble telescope isn't even parallax free. So do you really think a personal scope will pass that test?

Eliminating Parallax

If you have a scope that is lacking the extra dials to align focal planes, you are not completely out of luck. If the scope is a red dot scope that will allow the viewing of your iron sights through the scope, you are really in good shape.

Several scope-mount manufacturers push mounting options that place the reticle of the scope high above your iron sights... or iron sight manufacturers build folding sights to get them out of your way.

I personally prefer to have my front sight up at all times, which in turn pushes me to align the dot on top of the front sight. Of course, the front sight will always be in your way... yep, and I don't even notice it is there. I naturally place the dot on the iron sight and whack away.

How Does it Work?

Having the front sight aligned with your dot, assuming that your iron sights are zeroed to the same yard line as your red dot, will force you to attain somewhat of the same stock to cheekweld that we are always pushing for. If you are in a nonstandard position, a stock to cheekweld may be totally out of the question. Therefore, having the ability to align the front sight with the dot can vastly improve your chances of hitting the target. After all, that is what shooting is all about.

Using this technique will also help to decrease group size during your normal zeroing process. This will help you attain a true zero that will be consistent as you shoot from obscure positions.

Don't be fooled by the distance. Up close and personal causes shooters to quit looking at their sights and succumb to point shooting, which is a huge no-go. When they do finally pick up a set of sights to use, they place the sights where they want the bullet to impact, another no-go at these breath-smelling distances.

Now that you have enough information to get you through your next practice session on the range, you are one step closer to becoming a true combat marksman.

Top left: Proper stock to cheekweld, sights aligned on the target—the ideal situation. Top right: As the shooter moves his head, you can see the red dot move on the target. This is parallax. Head held to the left. Bottom left: Head held to the right. Bottom right: With the front sight up, you can cowitness and help to eliminate parallax.

HUNTING HIGH ANGLES

BY SGM KYLE LAMB (RET.)

INVARIABLY, WHILE HANGing around hunting camps, the age-old question of shooting uphill or downhill comes up. I always ask, *"Do you hold high or low?"*

The good thing about this question is you have a 50/50 chance of getting it right. The correct answer is that as far as elevation is concerned, you hold for the horizontal range, not the line of sight or actual distance from you to the animal. You are compensating for an unknown angle and unknown distance. There are a few ways to figure out where you should hold or what you should dial on your scope.

The first technique is to estimate the distance and the angle, then using cosines, determine what you should hold. Here is an example: 300 yards from you to your target, straight line. If you happen to have a 30-degree angle, you will take 300 and multiply this by .87 (this is the cosine for a 30-degree angle). The answer is 261 yards. If you are using a cartridge that shoots relatively flat, this may not affect you at all; however, if you were shooting .308 Winchester, you would have a 10½-inch drop from 200 to 300 yards. This is definitely enough to cause a wounded or missed animal.

The second technique is to use existing tools to ensure your success. Whether I am hunting antelope in sagebrush or elk on a mountainside, I need to know my range. That being said, if I have a Leupold RX-1000 TBR Rangefinder, all of these calculations are made for me. There is no issue with my South Dakota mathematics education getting in the way of hitting what I am shooting. I simply range the target and receive a True Ballistic Range, dial or hold the elevation and squeeze the trigger with confidence.

The second issue I encounter in steep country is not being stable while shooting from a scree-covered slope. If I get into the prone position I usually won't be able to see the animal or I will have to crane my neck, putting me in an awkward position.

Here are a few positions that may help you on the next hillside hunt.

SITTING POSITION with your knee supporting the rifle. This position has several advantages. First, you can stay in this position for a long time; if you are glassing or just sitting, you won't cramp up. You also have the ability to move your rifle to the left or right while in position; this is almost impossible when shooting from prone on a steep mountainside.

There are a few tricks that go along with this position. It is best if you have a sling on your rifle to use for additional support. This also allows you to glass and transition to the weapon without moving much or making too much noise. During our high-angle courses we routinely shoot and hit easily out to 600 yards from this position. You should also attempt to get your strong-side elbow on your strong-side leg if possible. This is often not possible, but you may be in a position to make this happen—the more meat on the gun the better. Don't let the rifle balance on your knee; wrap your support-side arm around your leg and squeeze the rifle to the inside of your knee.

KNEELING POSITION with your shooting side knee up and used in conjunction with your elbow for support. This position only works well if you have something to support the front of your rifle. A great example of this would be shooting sticks. More times than not, I see hunters carry shooting sticks for days on end, but when it is time to employ them they get it all wrong. If you only support the front of the rifle, you are totally missing out on the increased accuracy the sticks offer. Drop your support-side knee, raise your strong-side knee and apply pressure with your elbow to the top or front of this knee. If you have a long bipod, this will also work well when using that type of device.

If you are in the timber, you always have the opportunity to support the front of the weapon with the side of a tree or deadfall, just make sure you do not touch the barrel of your rifle to the support. At close range it

Supporting the front of the rifle with a deadfall while supporting the rear of the rifle with the elbow in front of the knee can improve stability. These positions should be practiced before going afield.

SPECIFICATIONS
POF USA P308

TYPE	Semiauto, regulated gas-piston operation
CALIBER	.308 Win.
CAPACITY	5 or 25 rds.
BARREL	16.5 in.
OVERALL LENGTH	34.75 in. (collapsed), 38 in. (extended)
WEIGHT	9.04 lbs.
STOCK	VLTOR EMod
GRIP	ERGO SureGrip or Magpul
FINISH	O.D. green CeraKote
TRIGGER	4.5 lbs., Tactical Integrated Trigger System, single stage
MSRP	$2,399–$2,549 for updated P308 Edge model
MANUFAC-TURER	POF USA pof-usa.com 623-561-9572

MARKED FOR LIFE

As a retired Special Forces soldier, I am completely comfortable with the ergonomics of the AR-type rifle. This comfort became confidence as I headed to Wyoming to hunt elk and antelope. Not only was I hunting with an AR, I was using a POF (Patriot Ordnance Factory) P308. And not only did I have a P308, I was hunting with the personal rifle of Frank DeSomma, owner of POF USA.

When I was cramped for time ahead of my hunt in receiving a rifle I had ordered, Frank sent me his personal rifle and freshened it up by replacing the barrel. After scoring an elk and antelope, I made that rifle mine on the condition that he sign the magazine well. Thanks, Frank.

won't matter, but at 100 yards and beyond, this can result in feet of deviation. Yes, *feet*—not just inches.

STACKING YOUR FEET is another position that you should practice before heading out the door to your next hunt. Although this position looks crazy, it works exceptionally well. Not uphill, only downhill. Lean forward; stack your support-side foot on top of your strong-side toe. Making sure the barrel is not touching your toe, grab the bottom of your foot and the sling or stock

and enjoy the ride. This is my favorite position for angled shooting. Don't be fooled by the look of the position; you do not have to be limber to get into this position.

You will be amazed at how well these positions work in the field. You may have issues practicing on the flat range, so sit on a hillside and see what works for you. You'll be comfortable, stable and confident when you have to shoot from a high angle.

❶ Sitting position with front knee up, rifle supported on knee.
❷ Kneeling position with shooting sticks. Note how the right knee is up with elbow pushed against the front of the knee for additional stability.
❸ Stacking your feet works extremely well. The bottom of the boot and bipod can support the front of the rifle. Don't let the barrel touch the boot. You should be using an adjustable sling in all of these positions for added stability, which will increase accuracy.

For some reason, the CMMG finish showed the pellet hits more than the other rifles did. But it kept on working regardless of abuse.

AR Abuse:
The Final Chapter

TORTURE UNTIL SOMETHING BREAKS.
BY PATRICK SWEENEY

After the last AR abuse feature, Editor Eric Poole and I took a meeting. "I'm tired of rifles surviving," he said. "I want you to do it again, and your orders are not to quit until something breaks." Ouch. I assumed he meant one of the rifles had to be broken, not me. So I set about asking manufacturers for rifles. I was upfront with them and said quite plainly that I was instructed to not quit and that they were likely to receive a box of busted parts in return. While I waited on the arrival of the rifles, I considered just how far I was willing to go. Very far, as it turned out.

THE CANDIDATES

For a more representative test, I wanted to get rifles from two big and two smaller manufacturers. The first four manufacturers I contacted sent rifles. Lewis Machine & Tool sent a CQB MRP in 5.56 NATO complete with its own non-folding but removable sights. LWRC sent a brand-new SPR complete with a perfectly detailed Cerakote finish from its inventory rack. I tapped Primary Weapons Systems (PWS), and they had a MK116 on the way before I hung up the phone. The MK116 featured a set of Magpul BUIS riding the rails. And for the last rifle I returned once again to CMMG for its carbine. You know the one; it's appeared in every one

of my other abuse features.

Since the last test, the CMMG has gained a set of Midwest Industries (MI) folding sights, an MI-railed drop-in handguard and a Smith Enterprises Vortex flash suppressor. Each of the other test subjects carried sights and railed handguards, so I left the MI parts on the CMMG. (Besides, I was curious to see how they would hold up.)

To keep things level, I subjected the first three rifles to the dirt and sand tests that the CMMG passed earlier as a preliminary qualifier to this final chapter. These rifles had no problem passing my earlier tests, so now we move on.

LET THE TESTS BEGIN

First the drop test. Instead of simply holding them high and dropping them, I climbed onto my shooting club's ballistic baffles and threw them. This required my climbing up the ladder with each rifle, tossing them onto the boards I'd placed up there for support and then hurling each 20-plus feet to the range floor.

After each toss, I'd climb down, load and shoot. That cavalier thrill wore off pretty quickly, so I started tossing them off in pairs or all four at once. They had plenty of opportunities to crash into each other. Somewhere along the way, I broke off one of the protective ears of the LWRC rear Skirmish sight.

Dropping rifles is one thing, tossing them out of the equivalent of a second-story window is worse.

Throw rifles enough and you'll eventually spear one into the ground.

Drop rifles into sand, and they get earth wedged into the wrong places. Do not fire a rifle with an obstructed bore!

The LMT sights are beyond tough. This one is packed with dirt and leaves, but a good crush against a post cleared it up enough. These sights still work.

The sight still worked, it just lost the side. I also had sand jam the flash hiders, which I "cleared" by banging the barrel against the baffle stand post. They all appeared to retain their engineered geometry and fired just fine.

Next, I chucked them across an old parking lot. Throwing ARs is not without its hazards. First, they weigh roughly eight pounds each, and they have edges, gaps and such that could maim you, so don't try this at home.

The way I found to throw a rifle that was safest was also the simplest: Wind up as if each was a baseball bat and then swing and let go. You can get nearly 25 yards out of an AR-15 before reaching one's physical limits. And if you throw them just right, you can spear the muzzle right into the topsoil. (That got me into trouble, as I'll detail later.)

After a few throws with each, I was making no progress, and test-firing was a bore. I tossed them one more time, which resulted in the spearing of the CMMG and its Vortex flash hider. Then I packed them

The wind-up...

...and the pitch. Well, the toss.

The LMT takes a hit, and this demonstration (and more like it) didn't stop it from working.

away. On the return trip, the packed soil had dried and hardened. When I next fired it, the dirt split the Vortex flash hider. The rifle and I (as well as my photographic assistant) were unharmed, but this incident was a clear reminder of how dangerous this type of ridiculous experimentation can be. I went back to the shop and installed a new Vortex flash hider before continuing, but I was a lot less cavalier about bore and flash hider obstructions after that.

A ROAD TEST OF A SORT

I ran over the rifles with my car: one side down, then the other, then lengthwise. I sent a teaser photo to Eric, and his reply was spooky: "A Ford Taurus?" he asked. How could he tell? "I was a very observant Marine," he said. "Not only is it a Taurus, but you need to rotate the tires more often; they're a few pounds low. And tell the club groundskeeper to mow one more time before winter." Right on all points. So I ramped things up and made a mental note: no getting things past Eric; it's not worth trying.

I invited my brother, and his 4X4, to participate in the next series. While he was on the way to the range, I spent my time throwing the rifles across the gravel parking lot. In the course of those throws, I managed to mangle the Magpul rear sight on the PWS MK116. It no longer worked as a precision sight, but if I raised it I could use the open ears as a rough CQB sight.

This time, we ran over them with the truck—all ton-and-a-half of it. This pro-

duced results no better than that of my Taurus, despite the extra weight and gravel surface. Well, it did add fresh scars to the aluminum anodizing and Cerakote finish.

While we were hard at it, another club member showed up in his truck. While he watched, wide-eyed, as we ran over the rifles, I considered his truck. A Ford F250 Super Duty V8 Diesel. Almost five tons of truck. Eric would be pleased.

Shooting a flash hider that's plugged with dirt will often produce dangerous shrapenel as a result. The lesson is to check your bores before you shoot.

After this man was convinced we were not pulling his leg, he unhitched the trailer and gleefully proceeded to drive over the rifles. And there we made progress. I could see the rifles flexing under the tires. In fact, it was becoming so interesting that we parked the truck on them. Visible damage? The finishes were pretty scarred. The PWS MK116, with its lightened and sculpted-for-cooling airflow forearm, had bent rails. The stocks were so scuffed up that it wasn't really fun to shoot the rifles afterwards.

On the first post-F250 test-fire, the LMT CQB MRP fired one round and stopped. Hmm. I opened it and almost ended up

A family sedan? ARs scoffed at this effort. After all, its curb weight is reportedly 3,336 pounds.

This is an idling F250 Super Duty V8 Diesel, parked on ARs. Ford says it weighs 9,800 pounds.

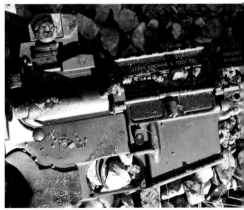

This is what ARs look like after being run over and abused. The LMT MRP has proven itself to be one of the toughest ARs ever.

Even after the left protective ear of the LWRC Skirmish sight was broken off, it still worked as designed.

with the buffer in my face. At some point during the F250 abuse, the receiver and buffer tube had flexed enough to allow the buffer retainer and spring to pop out and tie up the action. Once I shook them out of the lower and reinstalled, the LMT worked like a Swiss watch. A scarred, uglified Swiss watch. However, the front takedown pin was broken in two; it still held the upper and lower receivers together. (It just wasn't a captured part anymore.) The PWS? Despite the visibly bent railed forearm, the piston still shuttled without complaint. The LWRC and the CMMG suffered nothing but cosmetic damage.

THE ULTIMATE TEST

One rifle, temporarily sidelined, was not enough. So I unveiled the last test I would administer—I'd shoot them. No, you misunderstood; I meant shoot *at* them. If there is one thing we've learned from after-action reports of shooting incidents, it's that a lot of people focus on the threat, the weapon, and end up shooting it. Hands and guns get hit. Now, if I whacked any of these with a 9mm, .40 or .45, we all know what would happen—the test would be over. So, I thought, what about birdshot from a shotgun?

Honestly, I didn't expect any of them to pass and survive. So I test-fired them for accuracy before proceeding. It wasn't easy, with bits of gravel ground into the cheekpieces of the various stocks, but what I found was impressive: accuracy was essentially unchanged since

the beginning. They all produced groups hovering 1 MOA.

On the next range trip I brought the shotgun and a case of shells. My plan was simple. Load a rifle, place it against the backstop, step back and then hose it with five rounds of birdshot. Then I'd test-fire the rifle. I shot the magazines, too, while they were inserted in each rifle.

First, the LMT, with a USGI magazine in place. The first five shots of birdshot didn't cause any problems. I tried closing the ejection port cover, but the first shot popped it open each time. I gave up on that. The second series of five 12-gauge shots had driven enough sand and lead fragments in through the gaps. The action felt gritty, but it worked. By the end of the fifteenth skeet load, the magazine was so dented that I realized it was not going to hold more than 10 rounds or so ever again. And the LMT CQB MRP was so gritty it refused to work until I opened it up, shook out the junk, banged the bolt and carrier against a post and put it back together. Clearly, I had reached its limits. Also, clearly, the USGI magazine was toast at the end of the box of shells.

Second was the PWS MK116, and I inserted its PMAG in place. The first five shotgun hits produced no problems, but the second set finally produced results. On the first round fired after the birdshot, the PWS bolt was wedged rearward. A close inspection showed that a single pellet had struck the fluted PWS buffer tube directly on the thinnest part, the center of a flute, and put a hole through the tube's wall. The buffer

Even with gravel wedged between the charging handle, the CMMG still works

LWRC and the Cerakote finish held up superbly. I fully expected the finish to flake off when the F250 crushed it into the gravel. These minor scuffs are as bad as it ever got.

The PWS MK116 suffered bent hand rails, but it still worked even after being run over by the Ford F250.

Magazines fared worse in the shooting tests than the rifles. The USGI and Troy (left) were rendered hors de combat, but the Magpul and Lancer (right) still worked.

Before I took the final step in shooting a 12 gauge at them, I first checked accuracy. Thank you for the 1 MOA groups LMT.

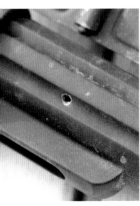

The PWS buffer tube and the one-in-a-thousand pellet hit that caused a temporary stoppage.

weight was wedged against the hole and the lip inside of the tube. I flipped the safety on and slammed the butt down on a post. The bolt cycled and chambered a round. The second shot, same thing. The third shot cycled. After that, it worked 100 percent—even after getting impossibly gritty.

The magazine was an interesting problem. It worked fine, but the pellets hitting the magazine body skidded up to the receiver, flexed the magazine wall and wedged between the magazine and receiver so hard that I had to disassemble the mag catch on the rifle, then brace a boot against the receiver while I pulled with both hands to get it free. Once free, it worked and fit.

Next came the CMMG carbine with one of the new Troy magazines. Things perked along until I had finished the fourth set of five 12-gauge shots. By then the magazine was battered and had holes through it, and that's when it refused to feed. Inspection showed that a stray pellet had penetrated the tube and broken the follower. With a ballistically created two-piece follower, naturally the magazine wouldn't feed. With a spare Troy mag installed, the rifle finished the test. Curiously, of the four rifles, the CMMG showed the impacts of the pellets more than most. I think the slightly rougher texture of the CMMG surface allowed more smearing of lead pellets, thus displaying hits more readily.

Last was the LWRC M6 fed from Lancer L5 magazines—the old-style mag, not the new steel wraparound version. Where

the others felt gritty, and were noticeably harder to hand-cycle when pumped full of shot, the LWRC SPR shrugged it off. The plating of the carrier had a lot to do with that, I think, as nothing seemed to stick to it during any part of the abuse. While the Cerakote finish suffered heinously from the impact of the pellets (the gravel had been horrendous to its cosmetics, too), the rifle wouldn't stop. By the time I was done, the LWRC SPR was so ugly witnesses were joking about it. ("Hey, it's too ugly to keep. I'll give you twenty bucks for it." To that I replied, "No, you won't, sir, because all of these rifles now have character.") The Lancer L5 magazine worked flawlessly and didn't crack under the impacts. They were definitely scarred, but it's still with us.

I'm convinced. Though new USGI magazines can be good, the best magazines to be had are made of polymer.

So there you have it. I managed to break rifles. I abused, banged-up, drove over and threw to their fates something on the order of seven thousand dollars of primo ARs, and in the end I found that they can withstand more abuse than any of us.

There are tons of factors that influence where cold-bore shots land. Many environmental conditions such as temperature, shot angle and elevation produce predictable point-of-impact shifts. These can be accounted for by inputting data into a ballistic program or gathering dope under different shooting conditions. But there are other factors, like shooting with a fouled or oiled bore, with a taped muzzle and in wet conditions. These examples are the source of endless debate. Seemingly, no two shooters will agree on anything, and that includes how cold-bore shots are affected by bore condition.

Over the past few months, I had coincidental discussions about these things with several professional shooters. Some always taped their muzzle, others swore it was an accuracy killer, one religiously cleaned his bore after practicing, and others never took a clean bore into a fight. After getting completely opposite points of view, I decided to spend an afternoon shooting and see if I couldn't come up with some constants. Some of the results were expected, lining up with tests I did years ago. Other

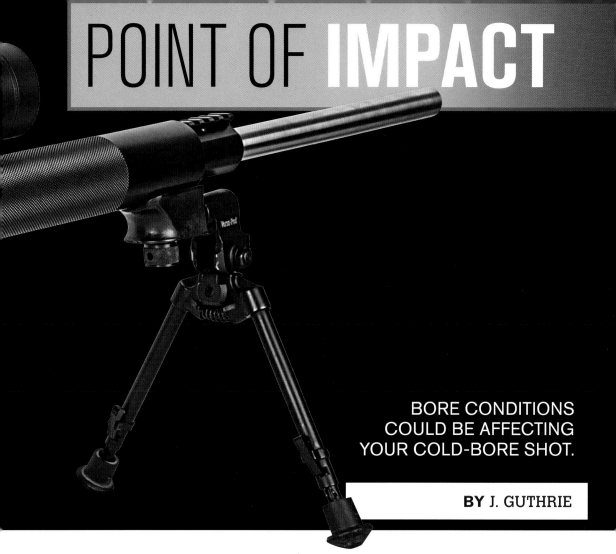

POINT OF IMPACT

BORE CONDITIONS COULD BE AFFECTING YOUR COLD-BORE SHOT.

BY J. GUTHRIE

experiments have forever changed the way I will look at a rifle's muzzle and bore condition.

TEST BED

Figuring that the differences in group size could be small, I wanted to use an insanely accurate rifle to look for increases or decreases in dispersion. A Les Baer Super Varmint .264 LBC-AR paired with a Leupold Mark 4 LR/T 6.5-20×50mm set in Les Baer's rings fit the bill perfectly. This rifle is guaranteed

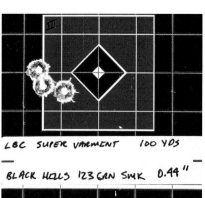

The best group from the Black Hills load was fired first, before the author tuned windage.

LBC SUPER VARMENT   100 YDS

BLACK HILLS 123 GRN SMK   0.44"

to shoot half-MOA groups straight from the box, but it routinely shoots a quarter-MOA group on my bench.

The Super Varmint starts with upper and lower forgings machined to specifications Baer spent a year perfecting. Riding in the upper is another custom Baer part, the LBC National Match carrier and bolt. A Geissele two-stage match trigger is one of the few parts on the rifle that Baer doesn't make in-house to his own specs. What really sets apart the Super Varmint from even most custom ARs is the 416-R stainless steel barrel, rifled in-house using a single-point cutter.

This rifle is one of the most, if not *the* most, accurate and finely finished AR-15s on the market today. I have close to 700 rounds through it, and it shoots well with just about every bullet weight, but it really likes 123-grain Sierra MatchKings, A-MAXs and Scenars. When Baer introduced his .264 LBC-AR, a slightly modified 6.5 Grendel, he arranged for Black Hills to load ammo. One of the two loads features a 123-grain Sierra MatchKing and is available through Les Baer Custom for $1.35 per round. Since the rifle will also handle the now-SAAMI-spec'd 6.5 Grendel, I also used Hornady's 123-grain A-MAX load (more on that later).

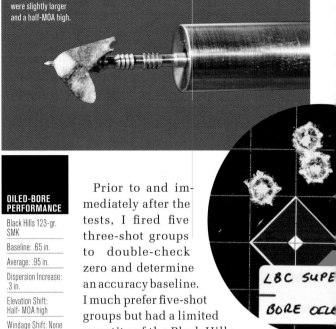

Oiled-bore groups were slightly larger and a half-MOA high.

OILED-BORE PERFORMANCE

Black Hills 123-gr. SMK

Baseline: .65 in.

Average: .95 in.

Dispersion Increase: .3 in.

Elevation Shift: Half- MOA high

Windage Shift: None

LBC SUPE[R]

BORE OIL[ED]

Prior to and immediately after the tests, I fired five three-shot groups to double-check zero and determine an accuracy baseline. I much prefer five-shot groups but had a limited quantity of the Black Hills load on hand, forcing three-shot test groups. Both loads shot to the same point of aim at 100 yards from the bench, with most touching or punching through the black-diamond center of my Hornady test targets. Prior to testing, the Black Hills load averaged .65 inch and the Hornady load .53 inch. Post-test groups revealed no statistically relevant change in dispersion, with the Black Hills load logging a .63 average and the Hornady a .49 average.

With an accuracy baseline, it was time to create bore conditions in the most consistent manner possible and see how the point of impact changed and if there was an increase or decrease in dispersion.

TEST ONE: OILED BORE

The majority of snipers I know prefer to shoot a fouled bore. Others, in the interest of preventing corrosion and theoretically extending their barrel's service life, are

The two loads used in testing.

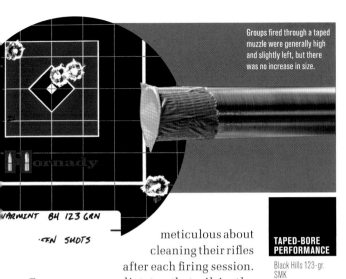

Groups fired through a taped muzzle were generally high and slightly left, but there was no increase in size.

VARMINT BH 123 GRN

·EN SHOTS

meticulous about cleaning their rifles after each firing session. Common sense dictates that oil in the bore would have some consequences, so the Baer's barrel was swabbed chamber to muzzle with an oil-soaked cotton patch before every shot.

Since the test target's black-diamond aiming point was divided by handy half-inch squares, it was a simple matter of counting the shots that fell above and below the centerline to see if there was a point-of-impact shift. Of the 15 shots fired with an oily bore, three were touching the centerline, two were below the centerline and the rest were above the centerline. Just looking at the test target, it is easy to see that the rifle consistently shoots about half-MOA high with an oiled bore. There was no change in windage.

Average group size with the Black Hills ammo increased from .65 inch to .95 inch. Statistically speaking, it's a huge increase of 46 percent. Practically speaking, groups were still under MOA.

TEST TWO: TAPED MUZZLE
This is one of those familiar arguments. Barrel taping has been a long-time staple for gunwriters, and articles on its effect on accuracy reappear all the time. Some guys religiously apply tape to the muzzle to

TAPED-BORE PERFORMANCE

Black Hills 123-gr. SMK

Baseline: .65 in.

Average: .65 in.

Dispersion Increase: None

Elevation Shift: Half- MOA left

Windage Shift: None

prevent water, debris and dust from entering the bore. The other camp can't imagine fouling this sacrosanct area of the barrel with anything, much less a piece of tape.

Most guys who tape their barrels simply shoot through it, claiming that the column of air pushed through the bore or gas blow-by ahead of the bullet breaks the tape, preventing any bullet interference. The anti-taping crowd has surmised that the same air column or gas blow-by would remove any debris or water collected near the muzzle.

I've gone so far as to argue that the type of tape is important, preferring electrical tape because it is more brittle than duct tape. Electrical tape breaks away from the muzzle more cleanly. Post-shot examination of electrical tape always revealed a nice, clean break, where duct tape was occasionally ragged. I've never seen the tape remain in place with a bullet hole through its center, an indication of just how violent things are at the muzzle.

Since duct tape can survive the perils of the U.S. Post Office and has held together everything from cuts to helicopters, I figured it would do a better job of inducing a point-of-impact shift and increasing dispersion. For every shot in this test, the muzzle was wrapped in silver duct tape and the bore sealed.

Amazingly, even to die-hard barrel tapers, I recorded no change in dispersion. The rifle's five-group average was .65 inch, the exact same as our baseline. What was interesting was the point-of-impact shift and how it changed the way the rifle grouped. Three of the groups had two shots touching and a flyer — if you can call anything in a group under .65 inch a flyer. The most consistent change was a half-MOA increase in elevation, just like the oiled bore, and a half-MOA shift left.

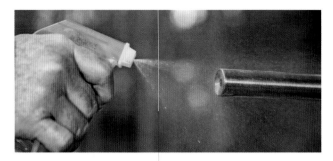

TEST THREE: WET BORE

Since it is impossible to make a bullet strike the same number of rain drops on its way to a target, I settled for moistening the bore with mist from a spray bottle. The condition replicates a situation in which water makes its way into the muzzle during a heavy rain or after crossing a creek or canal. My shooting partner, Jerald Allen, was kind enough to saturate the bore between shots by holding the spray bottle five inches away from the muzzle at a 45-degree angle and pulling his trigger once. The water was able to make it a couple of inches down the level barrel.

The results were, in a word, startling. After pulling the first target, Jerald and I were so surprised, we thought I had made a mistake and shot the wrong target square during the test. Three of the five groups were somewhat close to the target square, but two of the groups were close to five inches, with a couple of shots in each impacting four to five inches low.

At that point, I was running low on Black Hills, so I dropped some Hornady 6.5 Grendel ammo loaded with 123-grain A-MAX bullets into the magazine, found an accuracy baseline and shot the test over. Three groups later we had replicated the results. One group was more or less on target, but the final two groups went wild with rounds well below the aiming point. The first errant group put all three shots over four inches low, the second had a round in the target square and the final two low, one almost eight inches below the aiming point.

The wet-bore accuracy average for the Black Hills ammo was 3¼ inches and 3.86 inches for the Hornady. Obviously, the big surprise was the occasional four- or five-MOA shift in point of impact.

CONCLUSIONS & THEORIES

The good news is that out of three tests, two of the results were repeatable enough that a shooter could make a cold-bore correction and expect to be right on the money. As for the third test, it produced highly variable results, but at least the condition — a wet bore — is preventable.

For me, the test provided precious few answers and opened a Pandora's box of shooting projects. I would like to greatly

WET-BORE PERFORMANCE	WET-BORE PERFORMANCE
Black Hills 123-gr. SMK	Hornady 123-gr. A-MAX
Baseline: .65 in.	Baseline: .53 in.
Average: 3.25 in.	Average: 3.86 in.
Dispersion Increase: 2.6 in.	Dispersion Increase: 3.33 in.
Elevation Shift: Highly variable	Elevation Shift: Highly variable
Windage Shift: None	Windage Shift: None

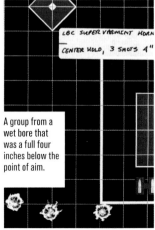

A group from a wet bore that was a full four inches below the point of aim.

expand the sample size and shoot 10 or more five-shot groups to check for changes instead of a paltry five three-shot groups. And you can certainly count on an Oehler 35P chronograph parked in front of the firing line to capture velocity data for every shot in future tests.

It's my guess that comprehensive velocity data would probably lead to answers for why both taped and oiled bores produced a slightly higher point of impact than a barrel in normal condition. My working theory is that both have slightly increased pressures that increased velocity. In the space of a rifle bore, a little means a lot, so a little oil would go a long way. And the taped bore hindering the air or propellant gases pushing out ahead of the bullet might be enough to raise pressures.

As for the wet-bore test results, your guess is as good as mine as to why a few shots (and sometimes entire groups) ended up four to five inches or more below the bullseye. All the bullet strikes appeared square on paper; there was no evidence of key-holing. Jerald was elated, now having an explanation besides his own marksmanship for shooting poorly in a rain-soaked High Power match 30 years ago. I canvassed a half-dozen serious shooters, most of whom were perplexed and baffled just like me. I've asked them to replicate the test and report their results.

Caylen Wojcik, a retired Marine Corps scout/sniper and Director of Training for Precision Rifle Operations at Magpul Dynamics, had the best off-the-cuff theory for the results. He surmised that since water doesn't compress — it just moves — and was unevenly distributed around the crown, the bullet suffered an unequal distribution of pressure as it exited the muzzle.

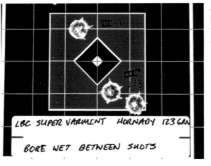

A group from a wet bore that was on target shows increased dispersion.

Best group from the baseline accuracy test for the Hornady ammo.

What operational cues can we take from this experiment? Marksmen should probably head to a final firing point with a dirty bore and a taped barrel. I'm sticking to the tape for the simple reason that it would prevent accuracy and point-of-aim-killing rain from getting into the bore. More important, it prevents a guy from turning his rifle into a very precise lawn dart by filling the bore with mud, dirt or snow during a fall — a mission-stopper until the rifle bore is thoroughly cleaned. If I was caught in a rainstorm without tape or a muzzle cover of some sort, the rifle would be carried muzzle down and checked for moisture before shooting.

DRIVE THE GUN

IT'S WHAT YOU DO WITH YOUR SUPPORT HAND.

Anyone nowadays can post a video on firearms training and tactics and instantly become an "expert." We all know that if it's on the Internet, it must be true. As it relates to firearms training, there is actually some quality stuff that can be gleaned from the World Wide Web. At the same time, it can be puke.

BY JASON TEAGUE
PHOTOS BY RICHARD KING

Let's address various techniques that are floating around regarding the use of the support hand and AR-platform rifles. I am stating in advance that this is not a definitive piece on the subject. Call it a primer if you will. This article is based on my personal observations and experience, along with conversations and training with people more qualified than myself. Understand that if a particular technique solves a specific problem for you, no matter how unorthodox it may appear, then more power to you. But we all agree that there are some methodologies out there that have been bastardized because someone watched a video on the Internet rather than having actually trained with credible instructors. Also understand that the techniques depicted are primarily applied while upright on two feet and/or moving and shooting. Although, done correctly, the C-clamp, or thumb-over-

The practice of placing the support hand out toward the muzzle has been around in various shooting disciplines for years. Controlling the muzzle in a dynamic environment allows for quick, controlled movements. Locking out the support elbow and sliding the thumb and/or pointing the index finger is one method that allows for solid control.

The idea of the support hand being held out closer to the muzzle primarily as **a way to control recoil is a myth.**

bore, technique that will be discussed works quite well while shooting prone.

ORIGINS

Who can say how or where the trend of moving the support hand farther and farther toward the muzzle began? Trap and skeet shotgun shooters have for the longest time pushed their support hand toward the muzzle with the index finger also pointing toward the target. They have been swinging 30-inch-barreled shotguns for years and learned that to drive the shotgun on a fast-moving clay pigeon, you had to get the support hand out there to control the momentum of a long barrel. Competitors in 3-Gun have long been using a similar technique of running the support hand out toward the muzzle and pointing the index finger in line with the barrel to also drive the rifle from target to target. No matter where it all started, the principle of pushing the support hand toward the muzzle to help snap the rifle target to target and drive the rifle has pretty much become the norm for most serious practitioners of the AR.

There are several versions to examine and highlight the correct application of said technique. We will also consider some old-school ways and talk about the pros and cons of them as well. Understand that not one single technique works for every situation, and like any firearm skill, the more tools to accomplish the mission, the better. Looking at how your rifle is set up may also dictate how you handle things with the support hand.

FACTORS

Devices such as the vertical grip and the angled grips have also lead to different adaptations of the C-clamp, or thumb-over-bore, technique. Looking back on the original SOPMOD M4 rifles, one will see the vertical grip being instituted as standard kit. This was necessary because back then (because the rail systems were still carbine length, and by the time you put a weapon light and a laser aiming device on a seven-inch quad rail) you had no place to really hold on to. So the vertical grip gave the shooter a way to control the front end of the rifle. Today you will find that longer rails are the norm. This not only gives you more space to attach accessories, it also allows the

The thumb-over-bore grip with a slightly bent elbow works well in multiple shooting positions, multiple handguard lengths and doesn't force the support arm into an awkward position. If using a vertical grip with any-length handguard, don't grab it like a broom handle. The tendency can be to torque the grip and pull the shot off target.

If using a tape switch, make sure that both hands can access the pad, because gun fighting is an ambidextrous sport. Running the switch on the 12 o'clock rail work very well with the thumb-over-bore technique.

shooter to get the support hand out toward the muzzle. I'm not sure if the technique of putting the support hand farther out drove the industry to develop longer handguards or if the competitive shooting circuit taught shooters who run-and-gun for a living to slide the hand toward the muzzle, but either way, it has proven its effectiveness.

The idea of the support hand being held out closer to the muzzle primarily as a way to control recoil is a myth. Each of these different techniques allows the shooter the ability to drive the muzzle with snappy, crisp movements target to target. The over-exaggeration of the thumb-over-bore grip has led many to think that it is to minimize recoil. There's no denying that the rifle is more stable while shooting, but the principle is to reduce the mass that is out in front of the shooter's support hand. The less weight or mass that is swinging target to target, the snappier and more controlled the movement of the rifle will be. If more mass is out front, the shooter will have a tendency to swing past or flock-shoot the targets. The muzzle must track target to target with crisp, controlled movements. If your given technique, with your particular setup and with your individual body mechanics, allows for snappy movements and, as a byproduct, helps control recoil, great. But the principle behind the C-clamp and/or thumb-over-bore technique is to drive the muzzle target to target.

Wrapping the support hand around the magwell while shooting in the dynamic environments that gunfights occur in will not allow good control over the muzzle. There's too much weight forward of the shooter's support hand to allow for crisp, snappy movement of the rifle target to target.

MAGWELL GRIP

Wrapping the support hand around the magwell has been around for years. The biggest thing I'll say about this technique is that while engaging multiple threats, it sucks. The weight of everything in front of the receiver is in front of the support hand. Trying to stop the movement of the rifle as you transition target to target is much more difficult with the technique. I'm amazed at how many shooters I still see hanging on to the magwell while shooting. Remember, I'm talking about shooting techniques, not holding a position for hours on end. And even if used while shooting sitting, kneeling or prone, the sling should stabilize the rifle, not your support hand grasping the magwell. Enough said.

TRADITIONAL

What I would call the traditional support-hand position is basically adapting a straightforward fundamental shooting technique from sitting, kneeling and prone. If you're plinking or teaching a new shooter the basics, then that's fine. But if you are training to be aggressive while shooting, or shooting at multiple threats, then simply slide the hand as far forward as you can and control the momentum of the muzzle. Again, we are talking about truly fighting with a rifle in a very dynamic environment.

OVEREXAGGERATED THUMB OVER

This is the one technique that just cracks me up and the one that I blame on the Internet. Basically, shooters have somehow seen (hopefully, not instructed) elbows straight out to the side or the locked-elbow technique and then took a left turn. I read or hear shooters talk about this technique of rolling the elbow up and wrapping the thumb of the support hand way over the barrel in order to control recoil. It doesn't! All it does is make you look ridiculous. This application also seems counterproductive,

A more traditional support-hand position obviously still has its place. Various kneeling, sitting and prone positions will utilize this grip, but if upright and moving in a dynamic environment, run the support hand farther out. Any particular support-hand grip is situationally dependent, and always being able to adapt to the need at the time is key.

as you have to fight to get into that position. It's not natural, and you are also blocking off some of your peripheral field of view. It definitely doesn't work with carbine-length handguards either.

LOCKED ELBOW

Many shooters run the support hand out as far as they can and lock the elbow. It is similar to shooting a pistol. Some use a thumb-forward grip or point their index finger, as opposed to the thumb-over grip, while locking out the elbow. This technique allows for good control over the muzzle while driving the gun, but it only works with longer handguards. It is also difficult to shoot prone with this technique. It works well on barricades and some kneeling positions. Shooting off your back or in supine prone are good examples of when to employ this method.

BENT ELBOW

I prefer the technique of having a slight bend in the elbow. This position allows me to shoot while standing, kneeling or prone. It doesn't feel awkward and works with a broad range of handguard lengths. I prefer to wrap my thumb over the bore, and in doing so, I can activate my tape switch on the weapon light. My mentor—and sometimes boss—Kyle Lamb, prefers to

use a push button on his weapon lights. I like the tape switch. The bent elbow can be applied from the strong and support side very efficiently without feeling odd. I am able to open the support hand and place it against a barricade or cover and stabilize my position while shooting. From the prone, I rest my magazine on the deck along with my bent elbow, pull against my vertical grip and shoot. Some of the other techniques do not really allow for a good prone position. I like the continuity of this technique from position to position.

YOUR WAY

Last, consider that when it comes to transitions, having the support farther down the handguard allows the shooter to get the rifle out of the way and clear a path for the pistol. With the support hand toward the muzzle, the majority of the rifle can really be moved quickly with less chance of the stock getting in the way of the pistol.

Again, these are observations, lessons learned and recommendations. There is no one right way, but there are wrong ways. Make sure your techniques are efficient and provide the correct results downrange. Spend the money and seek out training from qualified instructors, and stop trying to learn everything from the Internet.